THE LEARNING PROCESS AND SCHOOL PRACTICE

Chandler Publications in
Educational Psychology

DAVID G. RYANS, *Editor*

THE LEARNING
PROCESS AND
SCHOOL PRACTICE

May V. Seagoe

School of Education
University of California
Los Angeles

CHANDLER PUBLISHING COMPANY
An Intext Publisher   •   Scranton, Pennsylvania 18515

To all my teachers and all my students, who taught
   me what I know;
To my children, who taught me how much there is
   still to learn;
I am deeply indebted.

Contents

Figures

Preface

Teachers know what they want to teach. They know something of what the learners they face are like. But how get the learners to take in what the teacher wants to teach? The process is not a matter of content and curriculum; it is not an application of developmental psychology, nor psychology of individual differences, nor even the psychology of learning as a system of knowledge. It is the application of a set of teaching principles, gleaned from the psychology of learning, adapted to the content to be taught and to the characteristics of the learner. It demands of the teacher a kind of knowledge that tends to fall between chairs in our usual courses in curriculum and in educational psychology.

The Learning Process and School Practice is designed to supply that demand. It summarizes the learning principles that are common to all teaching, whatever the content and whatever the characteristics of the learner. It moves to illustrate applications of those principles in a variety of teaching-learning situations. It asks the reader to analyze the problems that confront her as a teacher.

The book therefore has a variety of uses. It offers exposition of the learning process for courses in educational psychology. It offers graduate students guidance in the psychological literature relating to principles of learning. It offers supervisors a method of analyzing how teaching may be improved. It may be used as a basic text or as a supplemental source in courses on educational psychology or in courses on supervision.

Each chapter includes certain teaching aids. The "Exercises in Application" present added applications of the principles discussed in the chapter which students may be asked to analyze. The "Suggestions for Further Reading" list reviews of recent research which the student may follow for further exploration of the basic literature; from these, graduate students may launch a search for the empirical basis of principles. The book concludes with a brief appendix summarizing the principles in the form of a checklist,

xv

"Implications of Psychology of Learning for Teaching," which may be used to analyze classroom situations.

In addition, any student using this book may usefully be given concurrent direct experience in analyzing classroom problems. She may observe teaching and try to pick out the strengths and weaknesses of a particular lesson. She may serve as a volunteer, presenting simple tasks to children and analyzing her own experience. She may tutor a child and try to figure out why he reacts as he does to her instruction.

The charm of teaching lies in this approach, wherein she may perceive each teaching-learning interaction as unique in specifics but related in general principles. Only the general principles are constant; what the teacher does to reach a particular learner requires continuing ingenuity. That challenge is what keeps teaching, and teachers, alive.

Foreword
By Malcolm S. MacLean

This book is a landmark. There is no teacher anywhere, or at any level from nursery to graduate school, who would not learn from reading it—not once, but many times—how to improve his teaching. A young neophyte who has absorbed the principles and practices Dr. Seagoe has set forth here will enter his first classroom better prepared and with greater confidence than those who have not. An experienced teacher will find in these pages answers to knotty problems that have long puzzled him, as well as corroboration of theories and practices he has found effective without knowing why they are so. And the scholar, psychologist, or educator, pondering the complexities and confusions of high-level, abstract learning theory, will discover many confusions have been cleared up. What is known about how human beings learn is mapped and supported by thorough documentation. What remains to be subjected to further speculation, exploration, and research is indicated.

The design and organization of each chapter is superb. It opens with a statement of a problem or a series of related problems common to all teachers and teaching. Take, for example, the question every teacher continually asks himself: What makes one of my students eager to learn what I have worked hard to give him, and makes another bluntly refuse to try to learn? In other words: What is motivation? Is there only one or are there many kinds? Does one work with one student and not with another? If answers can be found to these basic questions, teaching and learning in the classroom reaches an ever higher level of efficiency and satisfaction. Dr. Seagoe provides suggestions: first, by drawing together all the findings of research; second, by distilling from the research simply and clearly stated principles; third, by describing the specific application of each principle to the work of the classroom; fourth, by giving illustrations, often quotations from practicing teachers, of what happens when the principle is followed, and what difficulties occur when it is not; fifth, by furnishing a bibliography for those who wish to delve into the original sources.

In similar fashion the author deals with the bothersome business of students' forgetting. Most of us who teach have been shocked and horrified at the fact that learners who gave every evidence of having mastered materials before vacation at Christmas time or in June seemed to have little or no memory of them on their return to school. It is common to feel that we have failed in our teaching, perhaps that education itself is futile. Here again, Dr. Seagoe gives us solid research to show that a certain amount of forgetting is inevitable, normal, and necessary. But she goes on to show how, by application of sound principles through proved practices, memory and recall can be better sustained and forgetting reduced.

Many teachers, many writers on education, have in the past complained of the great gap between learning theory—as presented by researchers in the animal laboratories and psychological and educational research centers—and what teachers must know and do in the classroom to make learning effective. That gap Dr. Seagoe has closed not only for those who teach in the schools and colleges, public and private, but for those who teach personnel in business and industry as well. One evidence of this is found in the following excerpts from a letter written by a teacher-supervisor of clerical workers in an aircraft plant. She says:

"The principles of learning have been applied and are working well for me. . . . I have trained about twenty people for various clerical jobs of varying degrees of difficulty. In many cases the training process has been traumatic for both the trainee and me. I had assumed that all people think and learn in the same way I do, and had been giving too much material too fast."

[Since studying the principles of learning] "I have trained people for a job that required mastery of a great amount of what appears to be nonsense material, and in a short time. By applying the principles of learning I have cut the training time from about three weeks to less than a week.

"Without going into details of the job, which is rather complicated, the principles I found most useful in this case related to length and complexity of material, whole-part learning, spacing, overt activity, discovery, and forgetting. Since I was aware of the learning curve, I expected a certain amount of forgetting, especially over weekends, and was prepared to give needed supervision at the beginning of the shift.

"However, the greatest benefit was in my own approach. I was much more relaxed and patient. My trainees started carrying a full load of work the third night with a minimum of supervision. . . ."

Clearly, great numbers of teachers will be grateful to the author for giving them this handbook, this constant companion and guide in the complex, difficult, but rewarding task of managing the daily work in the classroom.

1

The Learning Process and the Teacher

Whatever our concept of teaching as a profession, certain kinds of information constitute an essential part of the teacher's professional training. Fundamentally, education is guided growth. In this sense it is inclusive, embracing all the activities of the child that mold behavior toward specific ends.

In learning to teach we must learn, first of all, about children. We should learn enough about developmental psychology and maturational processes to understand how children develop normally as organisms with bodies, minds, and feelings, relatively independent of the agencies impinging upon them. The ways in which individuals differ from one another are also important, from the standpoint both of maturation and of learning.

Second, we must assume a goal, a socially desirable outcome toward which education is to be guided. This goal is in the area of educational sociology and educational philosophy. The nature of the goal depends upon the society in which the school exists. It determines which of the developmental directions we wish to emphasize, and sets objectives for teaching.

Given the learner and the goal, we have two methods of influencing behavior. One way involves selection of the materials and topics to be studied; that is, the content of the curriculum. The other involves procedure or method, based on a knowledge of the learning process. In order that growth may be directed toward the ends determined by our social philosophy, we need to know how behavior may be guided or influenced through the ways in which we present learning situations.

1

The psychology of learning is concerned with principles of procedure as they apply to subjects or to objectives. It indicates how the teacher may go about teaching a certain specific skill. It deals with principles of modifying behavior, principles that are present in all learning. Knowledge of them will permit the teacher to devise an effective method for each new situation as it arises.

LEARNING AND OTHER FIELDS OF EDUCATIONAL PSYCHOLOGY

The interdependence of psychology and education has long been recognized. An overview of the areas that "educational psychology" covers will help to establish the setting for the study of learning.

Of primary importance in educational psychology is the study of maturation, or developmental patterns. Developmental psychology deals with norms (and characteristic deviations from those norms) for changes in skeletal structure, in functioning of the sensory organs, and in motor development. It is concerned with the maturing of general intelligence and special abilities in the individual, and with differences in these qualities among and within individuals. It examines the process of emotional and social maturing, and the childhood experiences which contribute to full development.

Measurement, statistics, and research design constitute a second area of educational psychology. These tools are invaluable in the study of behavior. Standardized tests are useful devices in helping the teacher understand the learner and decide how to meet his needs. Teachers need to know enough statistics to be able to read periodicals intelligently and to decide when a test score is significantly high or low. They need also to know how to observe free play, how to keep anecdotal records, how to make case studies, and how to interrelate all these factors in studying the individual.

A third area of educational psychology is the learning process. The study of this process shows how changes in behavior or knowledge or attitude may be brought about with the greatest efficiency. The psychology of learning is a relatively independent field, one that cuts across age levels and subject-matter fields to describe general truths. Once the teacher has an understanding of the principles of learning and some practice in applying them to representative situations, she can devise her own practices thoughtfully and analyze her failures constructively.

WHAT LEARNING IS

When we speak of learning, we are talking about how behavior is changed through experience. We are not concerned with the behavior alone, although we need to understand initial behavior in order to know how it can be changed. Knowledge of the learning process is essentially the understanding of how we can influence others to behave in ways different from those they have adopted. Fundamentally, familiarity with the learning process is basic not only to teaching but also to advertising, personnel management, parenthood, or any field in which we try to influence the thinking and actions of others.

Although fatigue also causes changes in behavior, fatigue-caused changes do not represent learning but rather a physiological condition which may lead to cessation of learning or even to temporary loss of material already learned.

Each period of life has its own learnings. The child at home learns to vary his cries, to sit up, stand, walk, talk, and climb. He learns expected standards of behavior and a degree of emotional control. When he enters school, he learns to associate the words he uses in talking with words that are written or printed, and to reproduce them—that is, to read, write, and spell. He observes quantitative relationships and represents them as symbols—that is, he does arithmetic. He learns many facts and attitudes in social studies, in science, and in the arts. Most important of all, he learns to exercise self-control without frustration; to work systematically, yet tolerate interruption; to evolve ideas of his own to which he is committed, yet tolerate different ideas in others; to play as a member of a team or be content to play alone; to take a lead in a class play or be a stagehand in the wings. Outside school he learns how to earn and spend money, to live with people his own age who give him none of the special privileges that families allow, to adopt a religious belief which may differ from that of his fellows, to plan a life beyond school in terms of work and a family of his own, and to relate in a useful fashion to his community and country.

In adults, learning is less authoritatively directed; yet from newspapers and magazines and movies and radio and television the adult is exposed to a constant stream of thoughts which reinforce or attack his points of view. He constantly meets new experiences in finding work, establishing a family, learning how to invest, taking a vacation, and meeting countless other situations. A major achievement is learning to adapt to old age, to retire, to distinguish the areas which age leaves untouched or enhances and to live fully in each period. To have solved all problems or to have become fixed in reaction means to have stopped living. Life is fluid, and response to it must be equally fluid.

THE IMPORTANCE OF A KNOWLEDGE OF THE LEARNING PROCESS FOR THE TEACHER

An understanding of the principles of learning is essential for those who plan to teach in schools. In this environment learning is the primary goal and the subject matter is comparatively limited. Here students in large groups spend many of their waking hours during important formative years.

Teachers must, of course, be well-informed adults, knowing not only the facts they teach but also the relation of those facts to the whole of human knowledge. Over and above their information, however, teachers need both an interest in and a technical understanding of their students as living and growing human beings. They need to know what their pupils are like outside school, what their homes and families are like, and how they may be expected to develop in their total life patterns.

In addition, the teacher needs an understanding of the learning process itself, the process by which her way of thinking becomes a part of the way of thinking of those she teaches. It is only by knowing how learning occurs that the teacher can guide growth. The implication of the verb "to teach" is that the teacher actively changes the learner's behavior. But actually all the teacher can do is to arrange conditions which, in the light of her knowledge and experience, are likely to produce reactions of a given sort in the learner. The teacher sets the stage and supplies the properties; the student is the actor in the learning process. *Teaching, then, is the arranging of situations in which the learner will modify his own behavior in certain ways.*

SOURCES OF INFORMATION ON THE LEARNING PROCESS

We have said that the teacher needs to understand the principles of learning, not simply how to go about teaching a specific subject. This need arises not only because teachers are often assigned to grades and subjects for which they are not specifically trained, but also because classes differ and because individuals within those classes differ still more. The need holds even though an expert supervisor is often available for help in selecting materials, for planning, and for instructing the teacher in the needed skills. Sometimes, indeed, the teacher will find a supervisor who will explain the scientific principles underlying her practices as well as their philosophical justification; but even the best, most analytical, and most available supervisors are limited in the time they can give to any one teacher.

It is helpful to realize that there are fundamental principles which underlie all teaching method, independent of content, and modified only in degree by characteristics of the learner and the content of the learning. The teacher learns these principles, not through being instructed in exactly how to handle more and more situations, but through incorporating into her teaching experience the information and generalizations acquired from reading experimental literature on the learning process. Thus, as the teacher develops specific procedures, she will generalize from them and so discover underlying principles. For example, she may see not only that context must be stressed in teaching long division or reading, but she may generalize further that meaning is an important facilitating factor in presenting social studies and written language—in fact, in all learning. Her learning process, like that of the children, is essentially one of induction, conscious transfer, and deduction, proceeding in the manner diagramed.

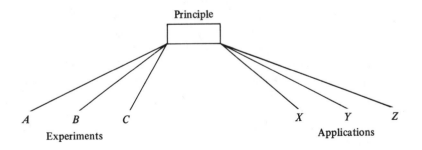

Experimental studies A, B, and C show a fundamental principle common to all three learning situations. The teacher evolves a principle from them, then analyzes practical situations X, Y, and Z in terms of that principle and fits her teaching to it.

As the teacher learns more and more principles, she learns to balance those which operate simultaneously in any learning situation. Her skill in balancing their relative forces increases. Only as the teacher achieves mastery of principles of teaching can she become sufficiently versatile and adaptable to justify calling her teaching professional. With less than full understanding of principles, she is like a surgeon who has a standard list of surgical procedures without the basic training in anatomy, physiology, and pathology that permits him to devise his own methods and to meet emergencies.

RESEARCH METHODS IN LEARNING

Although all the methods of educational psychology are applicable to some degree to the study of learning, the experimental method is used most often. Some consideration of research design may be helpful as background for understanding terms and judging the importance of specific studies.

In the initial stages of investigation in any field, normative methods (simple descriptions of events) are frequently used. Accounts usually consist of a description of what occurs under carefully noted conditions and an indication of the principle that seems to be operating. It remains for more exact methods, such as experimentation, to isolate the principle from the many other factors that may have helped to produce the result.

In the field of learning, experimentation with human subjects is sometimes done in the laboratory and sometimes in the classroom. Studies in the laboratory isolate specific learning factors that exist in the classroom only as parts of complex forces; but principles derived in the laboratory must be tested under classroom conditions before their meaning is entirely clear. Classroom studies are more lifelike, but they often fail to isolate any single variable for study. Both laboratory and classroom experimentation are useful. Similarly, the same principles operate for both adults and children, who differ only in the maturity and experience the learner possesses. Ways of changing behavior are essentially the same in principle for both adults and children.

Animal experimentation is also a favorite resource of research workers in learning, because variables can be more strictly controlled than in experimentation with human beings. Fundamentally, the principles of animal learning are similar to those of human learning, with the exception of situations involving communication and other social behavior. Though this exception is important, there is a basic unity in most learning processes. Principles derived from working with animals can be tested with human beings under laboratory conditions, then with students in the classroom. In many forms of learning there is little fundamental difference between the behavior of mice and men, or chimpanzees and children.

ORGANIZATION AND SEQUENCE

A sequence corresponding roughly to the order in which the different principles appear in the learning process itself is used in the following chapters of this book. In highly generalized form, that sequence is illustrated in Figure 1.[1]

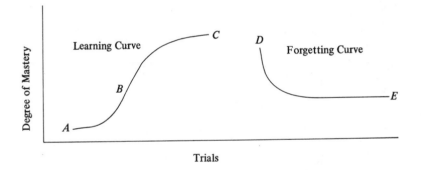

FIGURE 1. LEARNING AND FORGETTING CURVES FOLLOW TYPICAL PATTERNS

Section *AB* of the learning curve shows the initial stage in learning. In much of the teaching that is done in schools, that part of the curve often represents earlier learnings that have already become a part of the individual himself. Age, level of mental and emotional and social maturity, cultural background, and preschool and out-of-school learnings all affect what the learner absorbs from teaching. Learning in directly related skills and readiness for learning contribute to what happens at this point. Young children's

1 All learning curves are presented in generalized form rather than as the results of specific experiments. Further, time and error curves have been transmuted to mastery curves for simplicity.

learning to read English depends on their ability to speak English; ability to speak a language depends on experiences and their translation into oral symbols; having the experience in the first place depends on the maturing of sense organs and on the ability to interpret impressions accurately. Learning is a chain whose beginning always remains hidden, and whose end is never fully apparent.

Between B and C occurs the rapid initial rise associated with a new learning. It is the part of the learning curve with which the teacher in the modern school is particularly concerned. Here motivation or purpose has its greatest effect; the kinds of purpose that have been identified, their strength, and their permanence all have a bearing on the nature of the learning. The kind of material or the kind of learning situation is another fundamental factor; the meaningfulness of the material itself, its difficulty, and the sequence of presentation may help or hinder learning. The way in which material, once selected, is used is of equal importance; how to obtain the maximum intensity of impression, how to determine the unit of presentation, how to devise forms of activity, and how to decide when guidance should be given and when withheld affect the outcome. Such factors are discussed in Chapters 2 to 8.

At C the curve indicates the achievement of mastery. Mastery is characterized by full understanding, by repetition of skilled performance to ensure a high level of retention, and by conscious attempts to transfer the learning to other contexts. The teacher, at this point, is helped by having a knowledge of how to achieve transfer, of when to stop working on given material and begin a new unit, and of what kind of new unit to select, and when to prolong practice. Chapters 9 and 10 stress procedures which help to make learning permanent. Curve ABC combines AB with BC to make the "S-shaped" curve of the full learning process.

Section DE represents the forgetting that usually occurs at the end of formal learning. The level to which the curve drops at E depends largely upon the nature of the preceding learnings and the extent to which they continue to be used. Usually the drop is immediate. As forgetting takes place, the reproduction of what was learned is modified in predictable directions.

LEARNING THEORY

Psychologists tend to be preoccupied today with questions of theory, laws, corollaries, and the testing of hypotheses derived from them. In the future, when theory may have progressed to the point at which it has been completely formulated and its applications to the changing of human behavior have been tested, the teacher may be able to use that theory as a basis for devising techniques. When a teacher has developed the habit of scientific thinking, her approach to the unique problems that arise in practical schoolroom work is similar to that of the scientist who is testing generalizations in the laboratory.

At present, however, we do not seem to be ready with a theory that yields great generality, for our assemblage of facts is too small and too biased. Progress toward improved theory may well be made by collecting data showing orderly changes characteristic of the learning process, and by relating them to manipulable variables selected for study through a common-sense exploration of the field. Theories, thus, will be inductively created through slow merging of results from testing hypotheses of limited scope in a real world, where scientists of all sorts speak the same language concerning operationally defined variables. Such crossbreeding of psychology with other disciplines promises the greatest fruitfulness for learning theory, as well as for the specific disciplines concerned.

The teacher, however scant present theory may be, nevertheless works with a knowledge of learning principles; and these provide a set of tools to use in constructing a wide variety of learning situations. The rational superstructure erected on the basis of those principles is of less concern than the principles themselves. All learning theories have something to contribute. For instance, when we think of learning in the sense of mastery of set subject matter regardless of transfer value and individual interests, the explanations of the stimulus-response psychologists have much to offer. Alternatively, when we think of learning as problem solving and understanding and functional transfer, then the cognitive theorists are speaking our language.

In terms of the S-type learning curve, the early period of gradual rise is best described as trial-and-error learning. When the curve accelerates and rises rapidly, motivation and understanding and cognitive concepts explain what is happening. When the curve levels off again, the stimulus-response stress on repetition has meaning. When learning is discontinued and forgetting occurs, the cognitive theorist has the advantage in explaining the conditions under which learning is permanent and transferable to new situations.

We are saying, then, that no one theory of learning explains all the facts of the learning process as they apply to teaching, but that theories complement each other in placing emphasis on various aspects of learning. Accordingly, then, the essential knowledge comprises the basic principles of learning rather than the various theories which attempt to explain those facts. It is for the individual teacher to choose those aspects of whichever theory may best fit her understanding and help her practice, for that is the way in which she can best make the various theories subservient to the fundamental task of learning about learning itself.

EXERCISES IN APPLICATION

1. Are the fundamental principles underlying the teaching of reading and the teaching of arithmetic the same? In what ways are they similar and in what ways do they differ?

2. Do the principles of learning differ for children and for adults? What are the similarities and differences?

3. What is the role of fatigue in learning?

4. What is one of the major problems in using classroom studies for information about the learning process?

5. How can the results of experimentation on animal learning be applied to human learning? What is one of the greatest values of using this type of experimentation?

6. The learning curve may be described as a graph showing four stages: (1) a period of little learning, where skills basic to the later learning are being mastered, (2) a rapidly accelerating curve with much learning, (3) a leveling off of the rate of learning with relative mastery, and (4) performance, a relatively unchanging level of activity. At which stage is a normal seven-year-old in learning to read? A nine-months-old baby in learning to walk? A four-year-old in learning to talk? A fifteen-year-old in learning to spell? A twenty-year-old in learning reading comprehension?

7. Make a list of five or six psychologists who have formulated over-all "learning theories." How would you classify each: as primarily a "cognitive" theorist or as primarily a "stimulus-response" theorist?

8. Name two instructors you have had who have discussed the learning process. How would you classify each in point of view: as primarily "cognitive" or primarily "stimulus-response"? Why?

9. Why is educational psychology included in the basic training of teachers? In what ways do teachers use an understanding of the learning process?

10. If you were an advocate of cognitive theory, what type of classroom activities would you tend to stress? Drill? Problem solving? Pupil-interest groups? Detailed review?

The Nature of Motivation

Among the conditions essential to learning, motivation is one of the primary, yet also one of the most complex. The learner must want to learn, whatever the reason may be. Perhaps he has already developed an interest in a given activity because of pleasant experience with it. Perhaps he would like to increase his own feeling of adequacy, or to win praise from his teacher or parents, or to avoid their displeasure. Perhaps he wants to do better than a friend, or to please the class with his report. The essential condition is that there must be some unresolved tension or goal-seeking tendency. Learning does not occur simply by repetition of an act or exposure to a situation. There must be motivation; that is, the student must *want* to learn.

DEFINITION OF MOTIVATION

A motivating condition is one that causes the learner to start, to continue, and to limit his activity on a particular task. Motivation is a general term covering such conditions. An incentive is, more specifically, the object or condition which releases the general motivating force and sets off the learning pattern. In experimental investigation there are differences in the meanings of *motive, urge, set, incentive, task tension,* and *purpose,* but the teacher is less concerned with such distinctions than with the simple existence of motivation in some form.

Motivation in the general sense is a primary requirement in any learning sequence. Common illustrations are found in studies of the influence of an active attitude and self-activity on learning. All of us have experienced difficulty in remembering our own car-license numbers, or telephone numbers we call frequently, or exact titles of reference books, or names of people whom we readily recognize. These are experiences where we are usually not highly motivated. A vivid illustration is provided by a camp counselor:

I had been trying to teach one of the girls to row, but it seemed hopeless. She could not even coordinate the oars, or keep the oarlocks in place.

Meanwhile, I noticed that we had been carried out by the current beyond the lee of the island into a strong offshore current. I could make no headway rowing alone. I told the girl to take the stern oars and gave her highly specific instructions which she followed carefully. By the time we reached shore she was rowing quite creditably.

The importance of motivation as a general factor in learning is illustrated in the generalized curves shown in Figure 2, in which the incentive pattern for two groups is reversed, causing them to exchange levels of efficiency in learning.

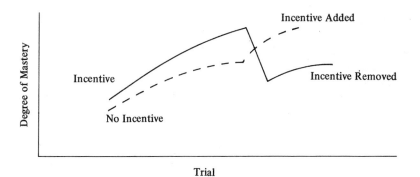

FIGURE 2. INCENTIVES INCREASE LEARNING

SHORT–TERM AND LONG–TERM PURPOSES

Sometimes purposes are long-term in nature; sometimes they are largely confined to the immediate situation; always they are complex. For example, the purpose of any student reading this book may be to gratify general interest in the subject, to draw from it some help in teaching, to get credit for a course and from it a determined goals in mind and group work will suffer from lack of common background. Instruction on what to look for or what to accomplish increases assimilation of the points indicated, and results in no loss of the additional marginal facts that self-instruction yields. There should be some form of purpose or "assignment" for every activity.

2. *The purpose should be made clear at the beginning of the learning process.* Questions can serve this function. The concept that questions should be used for examinations and for measuring the outcomes of learning has been modified; questions have a still more important function in setting objectives for work. Questions formulated early in learning focus attention on main points and promote organization of ideas around major concepts.

3. *There are many kinds of effective short-term purposes.* The teacher presents these as questions or statements. Perhaps the best statements or questions are relatively informal and spontaneous. The teacher will vary the technique used to fit each situation.

. . . IN THE CLASSROOM

One especially skilled teacher illustrates the use of an incident to build classroom motivation in an informal way.

My fourth-grade class is used to having a a "writing" period every day, and they love it. They write about anything they like, illustrate their own stories, and make individual booklets of them. Whenever they do not know how to write a word they either look it up in their spelling books or ask me how to write it.

We had been working on a unit on Chinese life, and I wanted them to do a little more writing on China. One Monday morning a boy came in full of energy and information. His Dad had just come into port from an assignment in the Orient, and brought with him a stock of stories which had entertained the whole family for the week-end. Seeing what we had as a resource, I quickly asked him to talk to the whole class about what his Dad had said. Of course, each child's family pride dictated that he must make an equivalent offering, and the tales were offered with enthusiasm if not always with veracity.

As soon as they were all trying to tell stories at the same time, and having a hard time to find listeners, I suggested they go to their seats and write their stories, that we would have time to read all of them later. They accepted the invitation eagerly, and I've never had a longer or more workmanlike writing period.

Unfortunately, it is not always possible to find such spontaneous short-term purposes. Sometimes the class needs a little drill, and the teacher takes more initiative in planning. Another teacher reports:

I take care of the drill problem in arithmetic chiefly by using charts. You know that you have to come back to a thing like multiplication or long division over and over again, each time for just a little while, if the children are not to forget all they know over a vacation.

Once every week we have a ten-minute "mixed drill" period. I try to use problems that everyone has learned to do, so that there are no new difficulties involved. With experience, I have been able to make them about equal in difficulty, too. We have a brief review of how to do the problem, give the children just ten minutes to do as much as they can, and let them correct their own papers. Then each child takes his arithmetic chart and plots his score for the day. Since there are always just ten problems, the plotting is easy.

I don't really care what their scores are. But by timing and by plotting scores a surprising number of children become interested in seeing that line on the graph slant upward. And making the problems easy serves my purpose in giving distributed review.

The teacher may also take the initiative by bringing in pictures or books to stimulate discussion, and in the discussion that follows the children may list the things they want to find out in reading. With older children and adults, a preliminary scanning of the material to be read may be followed by discussion and decision on important points, whereby individual reading may be focused on the central ideas. In more formal situations, questions prepared in advance by the teacher may define the purpose. In all these techniques the common element is the clarification of purpose in the beginning. The same thought carries over to planning units of work covering days or weeks.

ATTENTION AND DISTRACTION

In learning how to work with various kinds of purposes, we need to understand the nature of motivation. Essentially, a purpose narrows the field of attention and focuses it on smaller and smaller areas with greater and greater intensity. When we are in a state of relaxation, we are open to widely diverse stimuli and we engage in varied kinds of action. When a purpose that functions for us is introduced, we drop out the peripheral activities and disregard the extraneous stimuli; in other words, we give "attention" to resolving the tension or reaching the objective.

Some of the most illuminating material on the nature of attention is found in the studies of distraction. At first thought, distraction might seem the opposite of attention. Yet it is really spontaneous attention to the distracting element, given because the conditions attracted it and not because the learner consciously decided to attend. When we say attention is akin to distraction, we simply mean that some stimulus which we think should not be there has stronger attention-claiming power than the stimulus to which we think we should give attention. Where our attention goes depends on the balance of strength between that stimulus to which we think we should attend and the distractor which claims involuntary attention.

A number of studies have indicated the kinds of things people find distracting. Sounds such as a clock's striking or doorbell's sounding cause a consistent increase in the number of errors made and the time required for learning. The sounds of drumming on the table with a pencil, laughter, scraping chairs on floors, and whistling lower efficiency in spite of a favorable set for work and an increase in effort. Radio and television have a similar effect on quiet work such as reading for most children, though there are great differences among individuals in the nature of the stimulus that causes distraction. Noise that is constant or random, however, does not affect the level of mental performance of adults on simple tasks.

A second area of research has to do with compensatory mechanisms in fighting distractions, and with the levels at which they are effective in preventing loss in learning during distraction. Some investigators find loss in learning with any kind of distraction, such as a standing rather than a seated position, noise, flash, humor, lip movement, electric shock or threatened shock, or loss of bodily support. The loss is shown both in errors made and time needed to attain mastery.

Most studies show great individual differences in response to distraction and suggest the importance of helping pupils become accustomed to working in distracting situations similar to life environments. Others find that if performance is to remain stable under distraction, increased effort is manifested. Under distraction students talk louder, make more overt movements, vocalize, and in general expend more energy to produce the same level of performance.

If we generalize from the experimental evidence, it seems that:

1. *What the individual finds distracting varies with its newness to him.* The city dweller is kept awake by bird calls in the country, the country dweller by street noises in the city. Novelty claims attention.

2. *What the individual finds distracting varies with its depth of meaning for him.* Variety shows and conversation on radio and television programs are more distracting than quiet music for most people because of the specific attention pull of words and humor. Yet the person trained in music finds the distraction values reversed; to him, music is more meaningful than words, hence more distracting. In each case the stimulus with the greatest degree of association claims the highest degree of attention.

3. *Where the attention goes is determined by the relative strength of the competing stimuli for the individual.* When the learner is highly motivated for the specific learning, he has less difficulty than when he is indifferent to the task because it has no meaning for him.

4. *Whatever the nature of the distraction or its intensity, its counterpull takes a toll from the attention the learner is trying to give.* Distraction causes attention to be divided between the task given and the new stimulus.

5. *Performance can sometimes be kept at a high level under distraction by increased voluntary attention, but more energy is needed to maintain performance.* Muscular tension increases, peripheral learnings are lost, and eventually accuracy decreases.

6. *The level of distraction under which adults work varies with the activity undertaken.* Children should, then, become accustomed to normal adult distraction levels, thus making distractions less novel and less attention-compelling. There is always noise in a shop, or movement in a library, and we should help children become used to such conditions.

. . . in the Classroom

What effect do these findings have on the attitude of the teacher toward distractions, noises, and interruptions of various types in the classroom? The teacher may rule out most distractions by prohibiting noise and movement at all times and by requiring the raising of hands for permission to speak or move. This procedure will make for a classroom atmosphere that is apparently calm but actually tense because of the restriction of the learners' fundamental tendency toward activity. Or the teacher may exert little control and permit all sorts of educationally valuable activities at all times in the classroom. But if she does, reading groups may be disturbed by construction work, or conflicts between children may develop over competing demands for space.

The solution seems to lie in making the classroom distraction level similar to that found in the most nearly comparable adult situation. When adults read together in libraries, they move about freely, sharpen pencils as they need them, find new books, and even make occasional quiet comments to friends. They do not, however, do construction work or sing or engage in energetic cleaning up. Children's reading periods should mirror normal library conditions.

When adults saw lumber, or drive nails, or paint large areas, or work in shops, they move freely, with a high noise level. Children in their work periods should have similar freedom and should become accustomed to working constructively in spite of noise and movement. When adults assemble to discuss a question or listen to a musician or hear a lecture, they are almost completely quiet; children should learn this behavior, too, when it is appropriate. The school should help the student become accustomed to the conditions under which he will work as an adult so that he will be less easily distracted by normal confusion; but it should protect him from distraction levels which exceed the normal. By planning for each activity, the teacher can anticipate such problems.

Another kind of distracting influence causes concern to teachers: that is, unrelated interests or demands on the part of the learner. A child may be full of a story he wants to tell, or he may just sit down and scowl and refuse to participate. In such cases, what the teacher does will depend on her underlying knowledge of the causes of his behavior and the probable effect of a given action on him. At the moment and with the group, however, she will follow the principle of admitting distractions only as they are present in normal adult situations, postponing for individual conference those matters of importance chiefly to the person concerned. She may temporarily ignore the scowler and later enlist his help in another activity; she may ask the student who is full of his story to wait a moment until she is free, meanwhile sending him on an errand to discharge some of his energy. When disorder occurs she may wait until just before the next clean-up period or the next dismissal, then let the class discuss the problem and decide on an orderly procedure. In each case, the stress is on avoiding the diffusion of effort caused by yielding to distractions as they occur, and on handling individual problems without disturbing the group.

The school principal can do much to prevent distractions beyond the control of the teacher. If the class next door has a music period or a construction period or if children at recess play just under the window, it is difficult to keep a reading lesson going smoothly. If the principal calls on the school's intercommunication system at all hours, or frequently sends in notes, or uses a loudspeaker system by which he can without previous arrangement ask for the attention of the entire school, the interruptions consume class time and more time is lost while the class gets back to work. By planning to have the noisy activities occur in all classrooms at about the same time, by scheduling announcements so that they are given just before classes begin or just after they break up, or by letting the teacher choose her own time for announcements this type of distraction can be avoided.

Sometimes something unexpected happens to which the class must adjust temporarily. Perhaps it is a fire drill, by its very nature unannounced. More often it is a fire engine or an ambulance going by. If the distraction level is too high, the teacher may permit the class to follow the distraction and fully explore it, returning later to the learning. Few teachers can compete with a parade or a squadron of jet planes.

INTRINSIC–EXTRINSIC MOTIVATION

The terms *intrinsic* and *extrinsic* are often used to describe motivation, but there is much confusion as to just what is meant and much vagueness as to the psychological basis of the distinction. Furthermore, since *intrinsic* and *extrinsic* are used for contrast, people tend to assume that the motivation is either one or the other. But actually all motivations rest at some point on a continuous scale between intrinsic and extrinsic. And a motivation may be intrinsic-extrinsic in at least two ways: (1) it may apply to a life situation, in other words be more or less relevant (= intrinsic) or irrelevant (= extrinsic) to real life; (2) it may apply to the learner as distinguished from someone else, in other words may come from inside (= be intrinsic to) the learner or may come from outside (= be extrinsic to) the learner.

First let us see what happens when we define as intrinsic the motivation which is relevant to life activities similar to the learning situation. One asks whether a child will remember spelling better if (intrinsic) his correctly written letter asking for information is really mailed and he receives an answer, rather than if (extrinsic) he receives a prize at the end of the week for perfect spelling papers. In arithmetic, one asks whether he will be more accurate in arithmetic if his goal is (intrinsic) being teller for the class bank, rather than (extrinsic) earning the highest grade on his report card. In reading, one asks whether the child will learn to read more quickly by being asked (intrinsic) to read some material which the class needs, rather than by having (extrinsic) some stars pasted beside his name on a chart. In each case, there is a distinction in the relevance or the appropriateness of the goal to the learning that is going on.

Most studies of this type seem to show:

1. *The use of extrinsic forms of motivation is less effective than is commonly supposed.* It results in some added learning, but not in the large increases found when relevant or intrinsic forms are used. In general, the farther removed an incentive is from the goal, the less effective it will be. Conversely, the more relevant an activity is to a continuing goal, the more rapid the learning will be. Motives differ in strength in proportion to their distance from the motives normally functioning in that situation.

2. *Learning under extrinsic motivation tends to be temporary rather than permanent.* Extrinsic incentives temporarily increase output by increasing the effort expended per unit of time, but the only permanent incentives are the intrinsic, internal ones which permit maintaining efficiency during long work periods and a longer working life.

3. *The extent to which extrinsic motivation (as well as motivation in general) is effective is limited by the margin between potential and actual accomplishment.* For example, attempts to improve rate of memorization in accomplished musicians by using extrinsic forms of motivation are relatively fruitless.

4. *The effectiveness of extrinsic incentives varies with the degree of emotional stability of the learner.* The individual with a high degree of stability improves little under added extrinsic incentives; the disturbed student responds more to extrinsic pressure.

. . . IN THE CLASSROOM

It is clear that the more relevant the motivation used is to the child and to normal rewards in life situations, the more effective it will be. In addition, its transfer value to life behavior will be greater because the motive also transfers. Adults spell correctly in order to be understood, they do arithmetic accurately in order to get right answers or to hold a job, and they read for the sake of the ideas they gain and use. To rely on prizes or report cards or stars on charts in schools is to use motivational factors which drop out on graduation and also to risk having the skills linked to them drop out. Motivations used in the classroom should have a high degree of congruity with those operative in life.

The harmful effect of stressing extrinsic motivation is seen in an incident that occurred in a junior high school, as told by the teacher in charge.

In our school we took turns seeing that the auditorium was properly arranged and tastefully decorated for the weekly programs. My class had always done its part, gladly and even eagerly.

This particular week, I told them it was our turn again and asked for suggestions. It was early spring, and there were flowers. The class suggested that acacia might be a good idea, pointed out that there were several trees in the yard of one of the new girls, and went on planning the other arrangements on the assumption that acacia was the answer.

At noon, the new girl came to me, greatly puzzled. "How many merits do I get for bringing the acacia?" she asked. I explained that we had no merit system, that the class planned and carried out each job as part of its responsibility, but that perhaps she had not been sufficiently consulted and her parents might be unwilling to make such a contribution and we could certainly change our plans.

"Oh, no," was her reply, "it isn't that. They would be glad for me to bring the flowers. But where I came from we always figured out how many merits we would get before doing these things and sometimes it wasn't enough to bother about." It took a little while for her to understand we did things here because they needed doing, and not because of the merits earned.

Similarly, a stress on grades may have unexpected effects. Parents sometimes pay children for each "A" or each "Outstanding" that the report card carries, or promise a bicycle for a certain number of high grades. In high school, election to the honor society may be the goal. In such cases, once the bicycle is delivered or the society pin given, the hard work often stops. The goal is not to do good work but to win an extraneous reward which, once gained, lets the learning atrophy because its purpose (the reward) has been achieved.

Forms of extrinsic motivation most often criticized are the use of prizes (whether cash or candy or stars), grades, merits, and other systems of symbolic reward. In general, learning is adequately motivated by the life needs to which the subject is relevant.

Used in the sense of pertinence to the life situation, then, motivation should be intrinsic.

CHILDREN'S INTERESTS AS MOTIVATION

A second use of the term "intrinsic" has to do with the origin of the motivation, whether it arises from the learner or is suggested or imposed by the teacher.

A common misconception about modern education is that children always do what they want to do, and that their horizons are thus limited by the extent of their experience. Whether the child is interested in doing a given thing depends upon two factors: the amount of experience he has had doing it and the pleasantness of that experience.

The first approach to any activity is comparatively neutral. If an adult is asked whether he likes astronomy or horticulture or Borodin, he can answer only if he has had enough experience with stars or gardens or music to know what is involved. Because of the experience factor, interests of people vary widely. Attempts to list characteristic interests of children by age level are often misleading. Experience is the base on which interest is built.

If previous experience with the activity has been unpleasant, the learner will avoid repeating it. Early unsuccessful experiences with reading or writing or arithmetic cause the child either to avoid learning those skills, or to become so tense that he cannot learn. In such cases it is often necessary for the teacher to use elaborate detours and unusual approaches to get him to try once more.

On the other hand, if previous experiences have been pleasant, the child will want to repeat them: he will be interested. A positive attitude toward skills means that he will eventually read spontaneously in his own free time, will enjoy writing letters, and will figure out for himself when he will be able to pay for that catcher's mitt he wants to buy.

Studies of children's interests number in the hundreds, and the details belong more appropriately in the field of developmental psychology than in the psychology of learning. They include studies of children's play, conversation, questions, interests in school subjects, and response to mass media, to name only a few. The exact form the interests take depends upon the general culture into which the child is born, his friends and neighborhood and the opportunities they offer, and his own fundamental ability to succeed in various activities.

Although generalization is difficult in view of the complexity of factors affecting interest, the following observations seem justified:

1. *Children's interests result from their experience.* Children do not have native interests in specific patterns. Attempts to find games, books, topics, or other interest forms of universal applicability, or to impose a set pattern of experiences as conforming to an innate pattern of development, have little basis.

2. *Familiarity causes liking for the activity.* Sheer exposure to experience, provided it is not unpleasant, leads to the development of interest. This fact suggests that, if the teacher wishes to develop interest, simply introducing the material or the topic regularly in a neutral or pleasant atmosphere will tend to create a favorable attitude. Motivation accumulates through such repeated presentation, and the teacher can build learnings on the interest generated. The teacher has a responsibility for introducing children to new experiences outside their existing range of interests, thus extending their horizons.

3. *Success in a new experience leads to the establishment of continuing interest.* New experience must be fun. A quick, light, vivid, active exposure to a new area is the best way to assure that children will come back for more learning. The school fails in an important task if it permits the accumulation of dissatisfaction in important learning areas, or if it fails to build positive attitudes that will lead to later use of the skills it teaches. The dame school, in which reading was once taught with the help of the ever-present

bundle of switches, produced too many children who could read but avoided reading. The high school that requires formal teaching of Shakespeare for all students may produce adults who know, but avoid, Shakespeare.

4. *Among the factors that affect specific interests are age, sex, socioeconomic and educational level of the home, ability, and personality.* Moreover, any specific interest may be produced in different individuals or groups by very different forces.

5. *Points of appeal that emerge from studies of specific interests are:* (a) the opportunity for overt bodily *activity,* for manipulation, for construction, even for observing the movement of animals and vehicles of various sorts; (b) the opportunity for *investigation,* for using mental ingenuity in solving puzzles, for working problems through, for creating designs, and the like; (c) the opportunity for *adventure,* for vicarious experience in make-believe, in books, and in the mass media; (d) the opportunity for *social assimilation,* for contacts with others suitable to the maturity level of the child (ranging from parallel play to discussion and argument), for social events and working together, for human interest and humanitarianism, and for conformity and display; and (e) the opportunity for use of the new in real life, making the new continuous with past experience and projecting it in terms of future action.

It is clear, then, that when the terms "intrinsic" and "extrinsic" are used to distinguish between student-initiated and teacher-initiated activity, it is incorrect to say that all motivation should be intrinsic. Where the learner has interests, they should be recognized and learning should be built upon them. Studies of teaching such skills as reading, writing, and typewriting show that beginning with original composition about the pupil's own interests leads to rapid learning. However, the teacher's function goes beyond recognizing interests: it includes creating new interests. New and pleasant experiences, related to existing interests, will create new purposes.

. . . IN THE CLASSROOM

Now let us see how teachers use intrinsic motivation in the classroom. A sixth-grade teacher told of an experience in launching a difficult unit in which she stumbled upon a procedure that has many of the elements needed in building a new interest.

I got to thinking that we were using too many units of work that were interesting chiefly to girls, and that I should try something on methods of communication in order to enlist more active participation from the boys. But I was unsure of my own ability to make a radio, or even a telephone.

I talked with the supervisor, and started trying to make a telephone of my own before deciding what to do about the unit. I did it after school, and some boys discovered what I was doing. I tried being mysterious at first, so that they would not know if I should fail, but they soon caught on and began bringing in materials and suggestions from home.

When one of them asked whether they could try to do it, too, I discouraged the idea, thinking it might be difficult. It wasn't long until one boy brought me his instrument, made at home, as proof he could do it. From that point on the unit was launched, and I had to work to keep up.

It is especially important to allow for interest differences between individuals as students grow older. Letting children work on committees of their own choosing, with a wide variety of tasks, will let them use their interests to advantage. In a unit on communication, not every child will want to build a telephone; some will want to work on other methods of communication, or on reading for historical background, or on drawing sketches or plans or illustrations, or on writing material for a newspaper, or on preparing a class broadcast. The balance between using existing interests and widening them through exposure to new ideas is a difficult one, and the teacher must adjust it with care.

In brief, then, the form of motivation used should be closely related to the motivations that function in parallel life situations, but motivation may have its origin either in the child's existing interests or in new interests generated by the ingenious teacher.

IMPLICATIONS

From all these areas of investigation there emerge certain suggestions for teachers in handling motivation in the classroom. Briefly reviewed, they are:

1. Establish some kind of common purpose at the beginning of each activity. Recognize spontaneous interests; where possible build group activities around them. Relate each learning to previous interests. Make the purpose clear at the *beginning* of the activity.

2. Vary the distraction level in the classroom according to the needs of the group and the nature of the activity. Keep the distraction level lifelike. Relieve students of unnecessary distractions.

3. Use forms of motivation that are integral parts of the life situation in which the learning will function.

4. Develop long-term interests. Know and use the individual's existing interests. Develop new interests by introducing new experiences and making them satisfying. Build interests through using physical activity and through appealing to the desire for investigation, adventure, social situations, and realism.

EXERCISES IN APPLICATION

1. A junior-high-school counselor tried to explain to two classes why there was a foreign-language requirement for college entrance. One class consisted of very rapid learners and the other of normal learners. In which class would there be greater stress on intrinsic arguments? What would be the arguments for and against the requirement in each section, and which would receive more emphasis in each?

2. A sixth-grade teacher uses the period from 11:30 to 12:00 each day for spelling review and testing. Her room is just above the kindergarten, where that time of day is for rhythms, done vigorously to somewhat faulty piano accompaniment. Will this situation affect the ability of the sixth-grade children to perform in spelling? If so, in what way? What can the sixth-grade teacher do about the situation, assuming she does not want to ask the kindergarten teacher to make an adjustment?

3. How can a teacher decide whether there is too little or too much noise and movement in her classroom? What should be allowed in a reading period? In a construction period? In a class discussion? What over-all principle operates?

4. If the teacher wishes children to notice spontaneously some new material on the bulletin board, what is the principle she will use in deciding how to make up and post the material? What are some of the specific factors she can introduce to attract attention?

5. A local bank representative visited a sixth-grade class to interest the children in starting savings accounts. He described the process of opening an account and of making deposits and withdrawals. The children discussed going to the bank, using savings, and other related matters. The teacher changed her arithmetic lesson plans for that day to present the concept of interest. What learning principle was she using?

6. A parade is going by outside the classroom window. The class wants to look at the parade, but the teacher is explaining a very important concept. What should the teacher do? Why? Can you think of an illustration in which she would do the opposite?

7. What is the effect on learning of formulating study questions as a

guide to reading? Where should they be placed? When should they be formulated? To what principle is this decision related?

8. Enid, age nine, has shown a good deal of talent as a poet, while her sister Erna, age eleven, has high verbal skill but little poetic ability. The local newspaper offers a prize for the best poem by a child under twelve. Both decide to try for the prize. Which girl will improve most in her ability to write poetry in the course of the competition? What is the concept underlying your answer?

9. A bird whistled sharply outside a classroom where children were reading, and the children turned to look out the window. Would you call this an illustration of spontaneous attention or of distraction? From what point of view? What does this distinction mean regarding principles governing distraction and attention?

10. A professional violinist was quietly reading when his wife turned on the television to a comedian telling a joke. After a moment the violinist returned to his reading. After ten minutes of the comedian, the wife turned the dial and the Boston Symphony came on with Brahms' Violin Concerto. What will the effect be on the violinist? How will it compare with his earlier reaction? Why? What are the attention factors involved?

SUGGESTIONS FOR FURTHER READING

Berlyne, D. E. *Conflict Arousal and Curiosity.* New York: McGraw-Hill, 1960. A presentation of interest as aroused by gaps, uncertainties, and contradictions in the material presented.

Brown, J. *The Motivation of Behavior.* New York: McGraw-Hill, 1961. An integration of theoretical issues and empirical studies of motivation.

Egeth, H. "Selective Attention." *Psych. Bull., 67,* 41–47, 1967. A review of varieties of perceptual tasks which interprets research to show the process of mediating sensory input.

Jones, M. R., ed. *Nebraska Symposium on Motivation,* Vol. 1. Lincoln: University of Nebraska, 1953. An overview of theory and research on topics ranging from physiological processes to social theories of motivation.

Lawrence, D. H. "Learning." *Ann. Rev. Psych., 9,* 157–188, 1955. A somewhat technical review of learning research for 1956–1957 covering drive, reinforcement, incidental learning, rote learning, and retention from the connectionist point of view.

Lehmann, I. J. "Learning: III. Attitudes and Values." *Rev. Educ. Res., 28,* 468–474, 1958. A review of selected studies from psychology, sociology, anthropology, and education related to the nature, origin, and modification of attitudes.

Marx, Melvin H., and Tom T. Tombaugh. *Motivation: Psychological Principles and Educational Implications.* San Francisco: Chandler Publishing Company, 1967. An outline of the major efforts made by psychologists to explain the facts of motivation.

Paradowski, W. "Effect of Curiosity on Incidental Learning." *J. Educ. Psych.*, *58*, 50–55, 1967. A study of learning familiar and unfamiliar material showing the operation of curiosity as motivation.

Reed, H. B. "Anxiety: the Ambivalent Variable." *Harvard Educ. Rev.*, *30*, 141–153, 1960. A review of studies representing several theoretical orientations toward anxiety, emphasizing level of motivation in relation to learning.

Smedslund, J. "Educational Psychology." *Ann. Rev. Psych.*, *15*, 251–276, 1964. A somewhat technical review of psychological research in 1961–1962, including research on interest and learning set among other topics.

Travers, R. M. W., I. E. Reid, and R. K. Van Wagenen. "Research on Reinforcement and Its Implications for Teachers." *J. Teach. Educ.*, *15*, 223–229, 1964. A brief overview of 600 studies on reinforcement touching on definitions, intrinsic-extrinsic motivation, level of motivation, and social-emotional-intellectual forms.

Degree of Motivation and Level of Aspiration

Motivation is essential to learning. Its effect in narrowing the focus of attention has already been pointed out. It increases the degree of tension in the learner and produces a tendency to move toward a goal. Its function in the learning process is similar, whether the specific form is electric shock or blame, food or praise, time limitation or rivalry. The goal may be acceptance or avoidance of a specific condition, but in each case an increase in motivation produces an increase in tension and in activity.

A question arises, however, concerning the best degree of motivation. If a little motivation is good, is more still better? How can the teacher tell how much to increase the level of motivation? Is strong motivation effective?

A related question concerns how a given kind of motivation will affect a specific child. Does it matter whether the child really adopts the kind of motivation suggested? Under what conditions will he adopt it? How important is it that the goal should be his own, whether initially or by adoption?

DEGREE OF MOTIVATION

There is danger of inferring, from the emphasis on the importance of purpose in learning, that if a little motivation increases the rate of progress much motivation will be still more effective. Repeated praise, public reprimand, or making the child lose emotional control during a disciplinary interview are illustrations of some of the more intense forms of motivation teachers sometimes use. Let us examine the experimental findings with regard to level of motivation.

Studies of both animal and human learning contribute to our information here. Perhaps the most plausible generalizations are:

1. *Learning increases with increased motivation up to a certain point.* This generalization is especially true when the learner is working on a task well within his potential ability. Most of the evidence shows some increase in performance with initial increments of motivation.

2. *Maximum gain in learning occurs at a moderate degree of motivation.* Mild forms of motivation result in performance distinctly above that for no motivation, but strong motivation results in performance only a little better than that for mild motivation. In other words, there seems to be a negatively accelerated curve of increments in learning for equal increments in motivation.

3. *The point at which maximum gain in learning will be reached depends upon:* (a) the *complexity of the problem,* strong motivation having a positive effect on the solution of easy problems and a negative effect on the solution of complex ones; (b) the *ability of the learner,* motivation having a greater effect on those who have much ability in relation to the task; (c) the degree of *concentration of the motivation,* that which is presented in a number of small allotments being more effective than that concentrated in a single intense incentive; and (d) the *susceptibility of the learner to motivation,* that is, his tolerance for emotional stress.

4. *When tension increases beyond the optimal point, learning is disrupted.* In some cases the effect is satiation so that the learner no longer responds to the incentive. In some cases freezing or rigidity occurs. In others cases irrelevant actions for tension release take place. In extreme cases aggression against others may occur as a form of tension release.

5. *An increase in the degree of motivation increases the variability in a group.* Individuals differ more widely in their reactions under strong motivation than under mild motivation.

6. *Altogether, moderate levels of motivation result in the greatest efficiency in learning,* especially in problem solving. When motivation is very low, the learner is easily diverted by extraneous factors

and behavior tends to deteriorate into a series of acts that are not goal-directed. The effect of strong motivation is to decrease the quality of the work done and to increase the activity level. Under intense motivation the learner concentrates narrowly on the goal to the exclusion of features of the situation which are essential to the solution of complex problems. Moderate tension facilitates learning. The most effective motivational level lies somewhere between no motivation and intense motivation.

. . . in the Classroom

Perhaps a few examples of what happens under classroom conditions with varying degrees of motivation will help to clarify these principles. An illustration of failure of motivation through its overuse is found in a boyhood experience of a famous psychologist.

In the one-room school of my childhood I often had time on my hands. I would get the work done, and you know what happens when there are idle hands. I would devise things to do with my spare time, and they were often things of which the teacher disapproved.

One day I did something, I forget now what it was, and the teacher told me to stand in the corner wearing a dunce cap. I stood there for an hour, and the fun of creating a disturbance began to wear off. I stood there another hour, and I began to wonder when she was going to let me sit down. During the third hour, I figured it all out. If she let me sit down at the end of the third hour, I would give up that particular way of causing trouble. But if I was still standing at the end of the third hour she would be sorry!

Fortunately for the teacher, he was permitted to return to his seat at the end of the third hour.

The generalized nature of the tension created by over-motivation is also illustrated in so-called "sparking-over" activities. The motivation, too strong for complete release through channeling toward the learning goal, must find outlet in some other way. One young teacher told an incident in which a boy, unable to figure out how to finish what he was building, started rough-housing with his companion:

Mine is a second-grade class. We are working on a harbor project, with some children building boats and others wharfs and still others railroads and cargoes of different kinds. At the beginning of each work period we sit together and plan what we will do for the day, then each goes to his own work later.

Recently we visited the harbor near here, and found that the fishermen were planning a fiesta to celebrate the launching of a new ship. There were to be floats and steamers and a parade, and of course plenty of speeches. The idea caught fire in my class. Among other things they planned to build a small platform around which a fiesta could be staged.

Two boys volunteered to build the platform. It was to be one foot high by eighteen inches wide by three feet long. They gathered all their tools and lumber and got ready to work. They even had their rulers, the class having impressed on them that the platform must be the exact size planned. They didn't get to work, however. They picked up the tools, and looked at the wood, and talked, but nothing happened. Finally one of them came over and asked how to find out when a piece of wood was just eighteen inches long.

I was in the middle of talking with another group and, knowing we had talked about rulers in the planning period, I said, "Don't you remember? Just use your ruler!" He went back, they fumbled with the ruler and the tools some more, then they began hitting each other with the ruler.

What do you think went wrong?

A similar thing happened when a girl, unable to work out a problem in algebra, vigorously repaired her make-up instead. Even a teacher, finding that her day demands too much of her, may go on a coffee break and pour out her problems or talk of irrelevant things with another teacher. In extreme cases, aggression and fighting may result if the motivation is too high for it to be fully expended in the learning situation.

The question arises whether such findings about over-motivation are true only of negative forms of motivation or whether they apply also to positive forms. It is easier to find ways of making people extremely uncomfortable than of making them extremely happy, so the danger of over-motivation may be greater in negative forms. However, over-praise or constant success may cause over-motivation in that the child becomes accustomed to it and seeks it constantly.

A junior-high-school counselor had a relevant experience. She said:

I had wondered for a long time how to get a very bright boy to develop the leadership for which he was so well fitted. He was always among the top few in whatever his class undertook, but he always worked alone.

One day the class decided it would like to publish a monthly class paper. This boy was chosen as editor. The situation seemed ready-made for helping him to develop leadership. The teacher agreed, and all seemed well.

The next thing I heard, the boy came in harassed by all the work he had to do. In conversation I learned that he had written all the stories, was staying after school to set all the type, and was planning to personally run and distribute the papers over the week-end. I talked with him about the fact that editors have staffs, that others like to work on such things too, and tried to get him to let some of his classmates help out. Perhaps it was because he had gone so far in organizing it as a one-man job, or perhaps it was that he could not be content with any work less perfect than what he required of himself, but he refused all help and carried on alone.

I have about decided that too much success is as bad as too much failure. For the person who always succeeds, one small criticism has the unnerving effect of a major disaster. The boys who take criticism best seem to be those who are always in trouble, and are used to finding their way out of it.

In any over-motivation the child may respond in a stereotyped way because his feeling is too intense, or because he simply experiences feeling instead of continuing to learn. Somewhat similar effects occur with constant or overintense use of any form of motivation, whether it is knowledge of results, time pressure, competition, or reprimand. The danger that over-motivation will disrupt performance is common to all forms of motivation, though it occurs most often in cases of failure and emotional disturbance.

A word of caution is particularly needed for the emotionally disturbed child. Such a child is most susceptible to external incentives of all kinds, yet he is least capable of tolerating high degrees of motivation and at the same time maintaining the ability to think clearly under stress. Similarly, the mentally retarded child has a smaller margin within which to improve his performance, and strong motivation has a more disruptive effect on his learning than on that of the able pupil. For the emotionally disturbed and for the relatively slow learner, it is especially important that motivation be kept at the moderate level.

In general, then, forms of motivation which are moderate for the child with whom they are used are most effective in increasing learning. Under intense motivation, either the learner will learn to tolerate it and hence decrease his learning, or emotion will blot out thinking and therefore learning.

LEVEL OF ASPIRATION

Throughout the studies of the various forms of motivation, we are constantly reminded that students differ in their responses because the same form of incentive has different meanings for different individuals. No matter what the teacher may say, one student will take it in and respond, whereas another will seem to remain untouched. One will respond to the suggestion that he can contribute to the group because he cares what the group thinks of him; another may not respond because he is less group-oriented. One may respond to praise, another to an appeal for neat and accurate work. The effectiveness of any form of motivation depends fundamentally on the extent to which it has value as a goal to the individual. Students differ in what they value and in the degree of realism of their desires; that is, they differ in level of aspiration.

Much research has been done on the effects of ego involvement and of aspiration level on learning. Although the experimental results are most closely linked to studies of emotional reinforcement, their implications extend to those where emotion is the by-product of other forms of appeal.

Such studies seem to bear out the following principles:

1. *People vary greatly in their estimates of their own potential and accomplishment.* They underestimate what they have done in the past and overestimate what they will do in the future. If ability is held constant, level of aspiration is unrelated to actual accomplishment. Studies of intelligence test performance under strong motivation, for example, show that there is little improvement in test scores with increased motivation.

2. *There is a difference between what the individual expects and what he hopes for.* The difference is moderate if he is successful, but it becomes large if he is unsuccessful in meeting his self-imposed goals. What he expects is tied to reality to a great extent, increasingly so with successful experience in the task. On the other hand, what he hopes for is wishful, and remains independent of reality. He hopes for more as the task becomes more difficult and as he fails to reach his goal, and the more his aspiration differs from what he expects to accomplish the more defensive he becomes. The opportunity to rationalize and express his feeling of failure does not alleviate the feeling of failure or increase the realism of his estimate. Aspiration is not related to simple knowledge of the situation, but rather to self-image.

3. *Success in a task leads to realistic goal setting.* Those who have been able to do what they want to do will try to do just a little better, and succeed again. As a result they feel secure in achievement, self-confident, self-directing, flexible, and responsive. Success

brings the individual more experience with reality, and the reality he experiences is acceptable to his ego because it is the fulfillment of what he wants.

4. *Failure, on the other hand, leads to faulty and erratic goal setting.* The estimate of what the person wishes to do differs greatly from his actual performance, and from time to time. The individual may maintain his self-respect by a fantasy of success in the future greater than that of the most successful. Occasionally, on the other hand, he may maintain his self-respect by gross underestimation, committing himself to achieving even less than he will attain. Such behavior is associated with lack of self-confidence, inflexibility of behavior, unresponsiveness to reality, narcissism, emotionality, introversion, and sometimes aggression. The effect of both failure and success diminishes with repetition.

5. *The individual's sense of failure or success depends on ego involvement.* The same activity will bring to one person a feeling of failure and to another a feeling of success. High ego involvement brings the high level of motivation that is destructive to learning. It usually leads to frustration when any outside incentive is added. There is then a disturbance of perception and memory, and disruption of learning as a whole. The person must meet his aspiration or lose self-esteem. An increase of ego involvement, then, accentuates whatever neurotic pattern already exists.

6. *Level of aspiration is derived from parental expectations and group pressures.* When an average individual is told that he is doing better than the group, he shifts his aspiration downward, relaxes, and becomes more realistic. When he is told he is doing less well than a group, he shifts his aspiration upward, often far above what he can reasonably expect to achieve. The setting of individual goals is the result of indirect social pressures.

. . . IN THE CLASSROOM

The implications for the teacher are significant. It is her job to keep goals real and attainable, and to help the student to progress toward those goals. It is important that he be protected from social pressures toward goals that are unattainable for him, for such exposure results in reduced achievement and in frustration. Individually suitable goals, although they may be relatively low in terms of social prestige, must be made dignified and respectable in the classroom, and eventually in life itself.

Too often the child is taught that he may become President, or that he should hitch his wagon to a star, or that a far better world lies beyond the ranges. He is not told that the chances for the presidency are extremely slight, or that the hitching to a star results in a small motion forward rather than in flight into space, or that there is always another range beyond the one he can see. The result of such pressures is over-aspiration, inevitable disappointment for most, and ultimately lack of reality adjustment. Teachers sometimes contribute to lack of realism by building ideals of great material wealth and vocational achievement. Sometimes they more wisely teach the dignity of every vocation and the value of internal personal resources.

An illustration of over-aspiration is found in a perennial problem of counselors. In any class entering high school there are many times more would-be lawyers, physicians, engineers, and authors than can eventually be absorbed by society. More serious, there are many such aspirants who do not have the basic ability and interest patterns to make those vocations wise choices for them. The counselor has the difficult task of discovering suitable alternative goals and of gaining acceptance of those substitutes. Drafting or mechanics for the would-be doctor, arts or business or skilled trades for many others, are more realistic objectives. The pressure in our culture to attain more than our parents did is a driving force, and it is often directed toward the concept of the professions as the peak of the vocational pyramid. It is the task of the counselor to temper the aspirations created by society with some degree of adjustment to reality, and to build a sense of dignity and self-worth at the same time.

Such over-aspiration is often the result of social forces of which the parent is quite unaware, rather than of parental urging. One particularly wise mother once reported:

I had never doubted that our daughter was a normal, wholesome, fine girl, but I had wondered what it did to her to be born into our family. There was grandfather, up on the hill, the successful businessman and patriarch, with all his children gathered on his broad acres. There was an aunt who did a wonderful job of teaching at a nearby university, and the uncle just down the drive whose books were known everywhere. Not to mention the cousin who had been chosen editor of the yearbook and the one who was runner-up for beauty queen.

So I was an easy victim when my sister suggested that I let my daughter go to live with her for a year. There she did not have the support of the family environment, but neither did she feel its pressures. It is true that she failed to pass in a single subject that school year. But she did learn to think for herself, and she gained a social ease and poise that she could never have had here. We both felt it was a year well spent, for she came back home a new girl as far as self-confidence was concerned.

Sometimes making the over-aspiring person accept reality is a long process. A counselor reports:

One of my most difficult problems was with a girl, with intelligence in the low normal range, who had a sister in graduate school and a widowed mother who did domestic work in order to see that her daughters had all the best that schools could provide. The girl wanted to be a doctor.

When we studied vocations, I saw to it that she found out all about how many years it took for premedical school, how expensive medical school was, how few openings there were for women, and how few scholarships were available. I helped her to analyze her own grades and standardized test records, all of which led inevitably to the conclusion that she was in the lower half of her class rather than in the highest tenth. I suggested nursing or laboratory work or being a physician's receptionist; but no. It was physician or nothing.

She took algebra, and proved that counselors can be wrong by making a B. I began to think her conscientious habits and meticulous work might make college a possibility for her. So I began talking of typing as a means of helping her to earn her expenses through college. That she could accept, and she became a good typist.

The following year, when she came to second-year algebra, the picture suddenly changed. She was making D's in algebra, and a talk with her teacher showed that, although she could learn routine processes on a skill level, she was unable to follow when complex reasoning problems came along. She repeated algebra, and again it was D.

Only then was I able to persuade her to investigate courses for laboratory technicians, and only with the thought that technician might be a steppingstone to her first goal of being a physician.

There is the opposite problem of under-aspiration. Often the teacher will discover, with the aid of standardized tests, that a child is capable of accomplishing much more than he is doing. In class his work is mediocre, never poor but never particularly good. Nothing the teacher can do will seem to stimulate him. Sometimes the teacher, in desperation, will suggest he try to do the work of the next grade ahead, especially if he is old for the group (which is not uncommon). On checking a few weeks later with the new teacher, she may well find out that he is doing satisfactory but still mediocre work, a full grade above what he had been doing for her but still less than he might achieve. He may have set for himself a level of aspiration somewhere near the middle of whatever group he found himself in, and adjusted himself to that role at the higher level.

The problem of under-aspiration is crucial in many ethnic and socioeconomic minority groups. Financing further education can usually be arranged. Academic records are frequently adequate or programs available to meet specific needs. The crucial problem is that students feel that college and the professions are not for them. Colleges and potential employers are increasingly seeking out promising individuals in high school, exposing them to the college environment, planning with them for using their strengths and remedying their deficits, and encouraging a higher level of aspiration supported by success. Teachers in secondary schools particularly can encourage students of high potential whose aspirations are low and can put them in touch with agencies that will help them to continue beyond high school.

The goal, then, should be something just a little above the existing level of achievement, something within the child's grasp. If today he correctly spells five words out of twenty, his aspiration might well be six tomorrow, not a perfect paper. By building goals individually for each child, the teacher can help to make the child succeed, and thereby improve learning.

IMPLICATIONS

From these areas of investigation there emerge certain suggestions for teachers regarding motivation. Briefly they are:

1. Avoid over-motivation through too great intensity or too frequent repetition of a given form. Increase motivation gradually. Turn to other motivations before there are signs of disturbance such as turning away from the activity, freezing, excitement, or aggression. Discontinue motivation if there is any sign that learning is disrupted.

2. Help students to set their own standards for accomplishment. Avoid imposing goals that are foreign to them. Avoid adding to a strong self-imposed motivation.

3. Help students set realistic goals for themselves. Help the child

to know his abilities so that he may choose goals wisely. Individualize goals wherever possible. Dignify all goals so that each can retain self-respect.

4. Help students meet the goals they have set. Prevent failure by helping in the selection of suitable goals. Build self-respect whatever the achievement may be.

EXERCISES IN APPLICATION

1. A bright and gregarious boy in the eighth grade did outstanding work in all his classes, and became embarrassed because his teacher brought this fact to the attention of the class as a whole. As a result he was called "egg head" on the playground. What is likely to be the effect on his work? Why?

2. Pepi is a normal ten-year-old from a low-socioeconomic family, Foster a comparable ten-year-old from a high-socioeconomic family. Which boy is likely to work harder at learning to read. At excelling in sports? Why?

3. Rhoda was having difficulty with a complex problem in long division. Her teacher urged her to think it through, to refer back to simpler problems, to check the accuracy of her subtraction. Rhoda became more and more restless and flushed. What should the teacher do? Why? What principle is functioning?

4. A sixth-grade teacher brings to her class a book of ninth-grade reading level which has content that is related to a lively class interest. She asks for three children who will read it and report to the class. Are the chances equal that a slow and a normal and a rapid reader will volunteer? Or what will be the reading ability of the children who do volunteer? Why?

5. A high-school counselor was talking with a slow-learning student about his D's in Latin, urging him to drop the subject. He refused to drop it. His reply was that he would try harder, and expected to make an A at the end of the term. To what principle is this attitude related? What does it tell the counselor about the boy's basic conflict?

6. John's father is eager to have John do well in arithmetic. He is thinking of promising him a new bicycle if John gets A in arithmetic on his report card, punishing him if he gets anything less than A, or increasing his allowance so that John can buy the bicycle he wants. What advice would you give to John's father? Why?

7. A student with very high expectations is often unhappy with any grades less than those in the top ten percent. What is likely to be his response to the statement of his parents that they will no longer support him in college unless he can get a fellowship to handle part of his expenses, a demand that would require work demonstrating ability in the highest two percent of his class? What does this attitude mean in terms of

his ability level? Personality? Can you think of a parallel illustration for a ten-year-old? What does your analysis mean for handling such individuals?

8. Mrs. Jones told her fifth grade that she was going to give a standardized spelling test; that all whose grade placements were seventh grade or above would be excused from spelling for the remainder of the semester; and that all whose grade placements were below fifth grade would have to do extra assignments each week for the semester. What will be the effect of such a statement on the range of spelling-test scores? Why? What children will be most affected? What will be the nature of the effect?

9. What can the teacher do to help a child develop a realistic level of aspiration? To help the child whose level of aspiration is too low? Whose level of aspiration is too high?

10. Would the teacher have to give more attention to individual differences under strong or moderate degrees of motivation? Why?

SUGGESTIONS FOR FURTHER READING

Di Vesta, F. J. "Meaningful Learning: Motivational, Personality, Interpersonal, and Social Variables." *Rev. Educ. Res., 31,* 511–521, 1961. A three-year review of research touching on level of aspiration, achievement drive, intrinsic-extrinsic motivation, social factors, and other topics.

Irwin, F. W. "Motivation and Performance." *Ann. Rev. Psych., 12,* 217–242, 1961. A somewhat technical review of research on the effectiveness of various drive strengths.

Jackson, P. W., and Nina Strattner. "Meaningful Learning and Retention: Noncognitive Variables." *Rev. Educ. Res., 34,* 513–529, 1964. A summary of studies of motivational, interpersonal and cultural variables affecting learning including anxiety, socioeconomic disadvantage, and achievement motivation.

Krumboltz, J. E., ed. *Learning and the Educational Process.* Chicago: Rand McNally, 1965. A wide range of theoretical and research articles varying from discussions of motivation to computer models of teaching.

Mathis, C. "Motivation and Emotion in Learning." *Amer. J. of Physical Medicine, 46,* 468–479, 1967. A discussion of the state of knowledge on the relationship between motivation, emotion, and learning.

McClelland, D. C. "Achievement Motivation Can Be Developed." *Harvard Business Rev., 43,* 6–24, 1965. A presentation of a series of studies on increasing achievement aspiration in students from depressed areas.

Shaw, M. C. "Motivation in Human Learning." *Rev. Educ. Res., 37,* 563–582, 1967. A review of motivational factors intrinsic to the individual and those determined by learning context, including anxiety, achievement motivation, level of aspiration, and social-cultural factors.

Wohlwill, J. F. "Perceptual Learning." *Ann. Rev. Psych.*, *17*, 201–232, 1966. A somewhat technical review of psychological research on attention, reinforcement set, experience, sensory involvement, and related factors.

Wylie, Ruth C., and E. B. Hutchins. "Schoolwork Ability: Estimates and Aspirations as a Function of Socio-economic Level, Race, and Sex." *Psych. Rep.*, *21*, 781–808, 1967. A study of the relationship between socioeconomic level, self-estimated ability, achievement, aspirations, and parental and peer encouragement in grades seven to twelve.

Zander, A., H. Medow, and R. Efron. "Observers' Expectations as Determinants of Group Aspiration." *Hum. Rel.*, *18*, 273–287, 1965. A study of the relationship between observers' attitude and group aspirations in eleventh- and twelfth-grade students.

Forms of Motivation: Information

Granting that some level of motivation is essential to learning, that it should be related to the child's interests and to the activity, and that it should be of moderate intensity, the task of the teacher is to arouse and direct purposes so that a particular learning may occur. To do so she must know what kinds of purposes function best in classroom situations. The supposed learner may be failing to show progress in writing, or repeatedly painting the same picture, or daydreaming instead of reading. The problem is to know what forms of stimulation may be used to adapt his motivations to school learnings.

Forms of motivation may be classed in three groups: those which appeal to understanding or give information about the learning task and its accomplishment; those which appeal directly to emotion, usually through praise and success or through reprimand and failure; and those which function through the child's social contacts with other children. The lines dividing the three forms are fluid, and it is probable that all forms have some emotional component. To think of them in separate categories, however, may help to clarify the ways in which a teacher may act to stimulate purpose.

In the category of appeals through information there are two main bodies of research, one dealing with time factors in learning, the other with knowledge of results. Each of these is somewhat complex and varied in approach. In addition, there are many recent studies of programmed learning and of computer-assisted instruction which control these two factors, in addition to some emotional (or affective) reinforcement.

TIME FACTORS IN LEARNING

The teacher must often decide whether to set time limits for work, whether to emphasize working for speed, whether to urge the slow child to speed up and the quick child to slow down, or whether to introduce timing devices such as music or rhythmic pattern.

To clarify the alternatives and suggest some conclusions, let us try a little code learning. The task is to use the given code in doing substitution problems. Look at the example, in which the correct code numbers are with the symbols (page 45). The problem is to learn to do the additions using the correct number symbols. Have a watch with a second hand ready so that you can note the time you start and the time you stop. Do Group 1 of the problems, writing the answers only, noting the starting and finishing time. Check your answers before going on. See page 46 for the answers.

Now set a time limit for yourself. Do as many of the problems in Group 2 as you can within the limit you set, timing yourself as before and checking your answers for accuracy. See page 46 for the answers.

The chances are that you met your own time limit and completed all the problems in Group 2, cutting your over-all time over Group 1. This improvement illustrates the effect of time limitation.

Research is abundant on the relation between speed in learning and the amount learned and retained. Those who construct tests are concerned with whether the relative standing of individuals will change if there is no time limitation. A longer time allotment may result in an increase in raw score, but since everyone has a longer time all scores go up proportionately and individual rank does not change. For the average individual slow presentation has no advantage over rapid presentation. These findings apply not only to measures of immediate mastery but, in lesser degree, to measures of retention after a period of time. They are particularly true of material that is logical rather than illogical in character. The extent to which increasing the time increases the learning varies with the intelligence of the learner, his purpose in learning, the difficulty of the material, the opportunities for using external aids to learning, and the continuity of the context.

Experimental evidence on emphasizing speed as opposed to accuracy shows that, if attention is directed solely to accuracy, speed will gradually improve; whereas if attention is directed solely to speed,

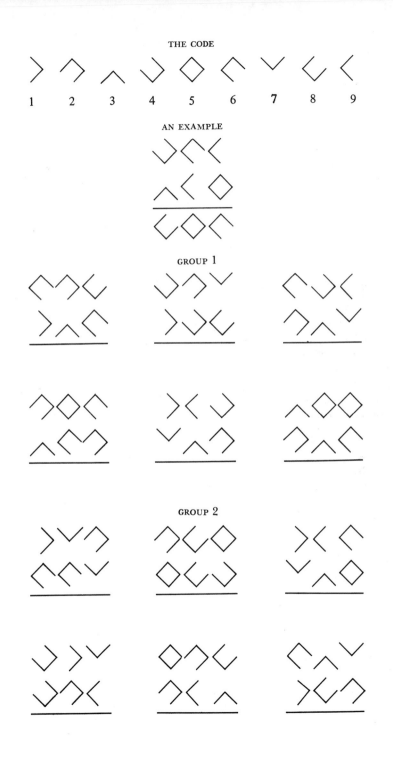

ANSWERS TO GROUP 1

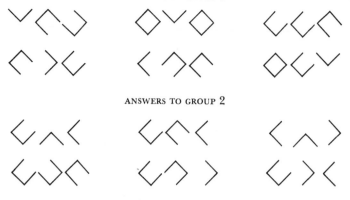

ANSWERS TO GROUP 2

accuracy tends to diminish. Stressing the amount of work to be done is more effective than emphasizing the amount of time available. Stress on both speed and accuracy is superior to stress on either alone.

Interruption of the learning tempo may disrupt learning. A constantly accelerated speed of presentation will produce less learning than a constant rapid rate. There is value in establishing and maintaining rhythms of learning within the grasp of the individual rather than constantly changing timing.

More recently, investigation has turned to the matter of personal tempo. Left free to set their own pace of work, children tend to adopt consistent rates to which they adhere. These patterns are consistent for similar types of work, although they are perhaps not generalized for all activities. Such time patterns appear to exist within the areas of speed of movement, reaction time, and speed of cognition. The extent to which they can be adapted without loss in efficiency is still unknown.

Such studies as these suggest that:

1. *The person who learns quickly also masters the learned material to a high degree and retains it over a long period of time.* Speed and accuracy in learning are related. The child who knows his arithmetic processes best will finish the set of problems first. The concept of the slow learner as characteristically thorough is not borne out by experimental analysis.

2. *The extent to which the more capable learner will be able to speed up is affected by how logical the material is, the intelligence*

of the learner, his purpose in learning, the difficulty of the material, the opportunities for using unlimited resources in learning, the continuity of the context, and the strength of the learner's motivation. In relatively routine and meaningless tasks there may be little relationship between speed and quality of learning.

3. *Setting some kind of time or work limit increases the intensity of work and hence the rate of learning.* If time is introduced as a factor in planning the work of the day or even of the next fifteen minutes, work will be more effectively organized and will produce greater involvement on the part of students.

4. *Speed instruction should always include accuracy instruction,* particularly in the early stages of learning. This approach suggests that accuracy is primary, and speed in part a result of accuracy. Even in later stages of learning, there should be a check on accuracy whenever work for speed is stressed.

5. *Left to his own devices, the learner tends to adopt a consistent rate* for problems of similar type. The rate is peculiar to the individual and relatively independent of intelligence. Urging a learner to modify his characteristic rate of work, except for brief intervals, will result in frustration for both teacher and pupil.

6. *Changes in timing should be used in moderation.* The effect of such changes as enforced rhythmic pattern, enforced delay at a critical point, or repeated change of speed show the same kind of effect as that discussed under degree of motivation. The initial adaptations, if they are easily within the ability range of the learner, result in somewhat greater tension and greater learning. If changes in time are often repeated or intensified, however, they disrupt learning.

. . . IN THE CLASSROOM

It is clear that the teacher should be conscious of time factors in every learning situation. Sometimes time limitation is accomplished through instruction. Or the teacher may say, "Let's see how long it will take us to finish these problems," or "In ten minutes we will see how many good questions you have on the material we are reading." More often she will say, "How much time will you need to do this?" or "Let's plan a time schedule so that we can invite visitors." In all these cases, time is being introduced as a motivating factor for efficient work.

The work schedule for the unit of work is an important part of planning. As one teacher described the process:

First of all we look at pictures and read and take trips and talk with people to find out what the unit is all about. Then we begin to list the things we want to find out, and what we want to do. For instance, last year in studying pioneer life we made a long list on the blackboard. We wanted to build a log cabin, spin and weave wool, make a covered wagon, learn frontier songs and dances, dip candles, and cook pioneer foods. It was a big order.

We remembered that we had only a few months, a few hours a week, to do all these things. The children suggested they divide up, and small groups work on different things. But nobody wanted to be entirely left out of anything. So we decided to work toward a "house-raising" put on for the parents as a culminating activity.

In order to make everything come out even and to be ready for the big day, shorter time limits had to be set for the candles and wood and costumes. We had to learn the songs and dances. The covered wagons had to be ready, and the sequence of action had to be worked out. Timing was certainly essential in getting all these activities to mesh properly.

Perhaps most of all, the teacher must expect students to work at varying speeds. A major problem in group work is that some students finish quickly and have time on their hands, while others finish late no matter how easy the task. Teachers handle this problem in several ways. They form small groups within the classroom, based on ability to do the particular job undertaken, and give the groups different assignments. They put optional assignments on the board which the student who finishes early may do. They assign continuing tasks, such as free reading or workbooks in drill subjects, at which students work whenever there is free time. Sometimes they individualize the work in skill fields, especially in the upper grades, so that each student may observe his own timing. Although individualization requires more initial planning, once it is under way it is easier to keep going than is giving the whole class the same work and constantly trying to adapt to differences in timing.

The teacher can consciously use interruption of accustomed timing for emphasis, avoiding such interruption when emphasis is not desired. Classroom details such as taking the roll, cleaning up, collecting milk money, and checking books and supplies can be reduced to a routine that will flow smoothly once the class is accustomed to the rhythm of that routine. On the other hand, planned interruption such as breaking into scheduled work to introduce a visitor or to present a book a child has discovered has value in emphasizing the new experience. The effect of the break in routine is to call unusual attention to that part of the learning. It is the teacher's function to see that such attention is attracted only when the learnings are of greater importance than the regular work of the class.

KNOWLEDGE OF RESULTS

The teacher must often decide whether to check a set of spelling or arithmetic papers instead of using the time to plan ahead, whether to evaluate paintings or seatwork or to assume that the self-expression is in itself sufficient, whether to take time to have students check their papers or to collect them and put them in the wastebasket. The learning being judged may be highly specific as in the case of fundamental skills, or highly variable as in drawing a picture. The evaluation may range from the checking of spelling papers to offering a subjective comment on a story. In all these cases the question is: How much value is there in having the student measure what he has done against what is expected of him?

Knowledge of results, in the sense in which we are using it, means the effect of the learner's being told (in any one of a number of ways) the extent of his progress from time to time during the learning. In a sense, knowledge of results is a part of all incentives in the learning situation, and it is therefore difficult to isolate its effects. It is also true that, although we may eliminate the knowledge we give, we cannot eliminate the subjective impressions formed by the learner himself. There are several studies, however, in which an attempt has been made to identify the effect of the knowledge itself on learning.

Another area of research is concerned with whether the information given should stress the errors or the correct responses. The contrast here is between punishment which is noninformative and stimuli whose effects are more informative than emotion-producing. We are concerned not with negative practice on errors but instead with the extent to which a distinguishing signal is more effective when it is attached to the right rather than the wrong alternative. Emphasis on the right response seems to be at least as effective for learning as emphasis on the wrong, and probably more so under classroom conditions.

In the interest of simplifying the experimental design, most studies of emphasis on right as opposed to wrong response offer only two alternatives, right and wrong. In the classroom situation (and studies thus far use chiefly laboratory-type materials) the selection is seldom that simple. When the teacher tells a student that he has made a spelling error, the learner knows he should avoid the word he wrote, but he may not know which of a number of possible alternatives he should next select as a possible right answer. In that kind of situation, giving him the correct response at once is more precise and more effective.

The results of such studies suggest several conclusions which have meaning for teachers:

1. *Practice without knowledge of results brings little or no improvement.* In the beginning there may be some increase in motor adaptation in a simple skill, but no sustained progress is apparent. There is slight evidence of latent learning, that is, of improvement which shows up under motivation after initial learning is completed. For the most part, practice is only a time framework within which other factors may operate; practice alone accomplishes little.

2. *Knowledge of results brings marked improvement in performance.* Evaluation is not merely a method of measuring teaching outcomes but is also an integral part of the teaching process itself. When a student is given knowledge of results after working without knowledge of his progress, his learning curve shows a decided upward trend.

3. *The more detailed and specific the knowledge of results, the greater the progress.* The learner needs to know not only whether he has achieved his goal but also how far from the goal he was and in what direction he deviated. Evaluation should be specific. Partial knowledge is better than no knowledge at all, but full knowledge is most effective.

4. *The more positive the knowledge of results, the greater the progress.* The reason for this conclusion may lie in the fact that knowing a given response is right is more specific than knowing a particular answer is wrong. Pointing out errors is less effective than pointing out correct responses, especially where the emotional content in the learning is moderate and any hint of punishment or reward is avoided. The effect of emphasizing the right response is that the learner's errors drop out. The effect of emphasizing errors is

that he still makes them but turns back quickly, a more roundabout method of meeting the situation. Pointing out errors makes the child remember the error but not its correction.

5. *Immediate knowledge of results is superior to delayed knowledge.* And the superior performance gained under knowledge of results persists after the giving of objective information is stopped.

6. *Classes and individuals differ in the way in which they respond to knowledge of results.* Young children seem to be affected more than older. Better students are affected most, whereas poor students are affected little. The degree of effectiveness of any incentive varies with the learner's estimate of his possibility of success in that situation. Further, the level of interest for the particular learner and the particular activity will affect the amount of gain from information about results.

The implications of these facts for teaching are clear. For most effective learning, knowledge of results should be introduced as quickly as possible and in as specific a form as possible. This fact probably largely explains both the efficiency of individual instruction and the inadequacy of imprecise letter and number grades. The information given, however, must be relevant to some motive of the student.

. . . IN THE CLASSROOM

Carrying these principles over to the classroom, it is clear that evaluation is an essential part of each teaching situation. Perhaps it is easiest to see the importance of this fact in the teaching of skills. When the student does an arithmetic problem or learns to spell a word, his work should be checked for accuracy, either by himself or by the teacher. Perhaps the advice of a training teacher is good:

Don't spend too much of your time checking papers for children. Spend it in planning new work, or on your own recreation.

Plan to check one paper in each subject for each child each week. Remember, the purpose is to tell you what to teach next, not to check up on the child. Ask for the papers without preliminary checking, and do it at irregular times, without announcement. By reading and checking you can get a good idea of how well you are teaching what you are trying to teach.

The rest of the time, have each child check his own paper. The main idea is to let him know how well he is doing, and what he should have done. Let him use answer cards for arithmetic problems; teach him how to check his own spelling paper by underlining syllables; let him rate his handwriting against a specimen posted on the bulletin board. Be sure he checks his work, but let him do it himself. After it is checked, collect it and glance over it, but don't spend your valuable time in constant correction of papers.

That she was right is shown in an experience of a student observer:

The teacher had taught a spelling lesson very well, I thought. The words were taken from a letter the class had written, she had presented each one in context and had the children write it several times, then dictated the words in a different order.

When the papers were finished, the children exchanged for checking. A boy near me was torn between trying to see what was happening to his own paper and making sure he missed nothing that might be considered an error on his neighbor's paper. When the papers were returned, the word "with" was marked wrong. An argument followed, the writer claiming that a small dash was a cross for the *t,* and the corrector claiming it was an *l* written near a blemish in the paper. Voices became loud, and they finally appealed to the teacher.

She handled it nicely though. Instead of giving a decision, she just said, "The important thing is that it should look like a *t,* isn't it? Suppose you write it again, very clearly." The boy did, wrote a heavy "100%" on his paper, and the air cleared.

Since the purpose in checking is to give knowledge of accomplishment to the student who did the work, self-checking or checking with the teacher is most effective. Having a paper checked by another child is no better in terms of knowledge of results for the one who did the work than checking it himself, and such a practice has disadvantages in inaccuracy and in disturbed social relationships.

Perhaps the best checking procedure is to have papers checked jointly by teacher and student. Then errors can be crossed out and the corrections written in, thus emphasizing positive information. The same training teacher said:

When you are checking spelling papers, cross out the misspelled word and write it correctly for the student. Have him rewrite the paper with the words correctly spelled. He knows well enough how to write it the wrong way; you don't need to call his attention to that. Provide the right word, and give him an opportunity to write it correctly.

The same thing is true of arithmetic papers. It is not enough to know that he has done the wrong thing. Cross out the error, and write in the problem correctly solved, then have him do it again on the reverse side of the paper. That will keep him from copying.

Or, better still, whenever you have time go over his work with him and make the necessary corrections, each time explaining why you are making the change. Then let him copy it in final form in ink. That will give him practice with the correct forms.

Keeping individual progress charts in skills, too, serves to strengthen the feeling of achievement. Spelling tests, arithmetic drills, and reading speed tests lend themselves especially well to graphing. The graphs should be individual, so that the student is competing against his own record rather than against those of his classmates. Learners differ so much in ability that a class graph inevitably leads to constant disappointment for some. Further, it fosters a form of competition that is undesirable in that the competitors do not have an equal chance to win.

In more complex skills such as writing stories, the same principles operate but the procedures for achieving them vary. The student and teacher together may check the accuracy of spelling, punctuation, and language forms. The teacher may make specific marginal comments on a paper. Perhaps teacher and learner will jointly judge the quality of penmanship by comparison with a scale. The teacher or student may read a story to the class for reactions on content and style. In oral language, the teacher may record the student's speech and listen to the recording with him to help him evaluate what he hears.

In less formal situations, as in the arts or in content fields, knowledge of results is also important. The seat work of children in the primary grades, such as reading games or clay modeling, may be evaluated through presentation to the class. The same thing is true of creative art, or of musical performance, or of the work done during an activity period, or of a problem in behavior on the playground. In each case, informal discussion by the class constitutes the best available form of evaluation.

In class evaluation, however, the teacher should show by example and by guiding the discussion how to give a constructive criticism. The effective criticism consists of three parts: a favorable or reassuring comment to help the learner feel secure in some area; an analysis of inadequacies or problems; and a specific and positive suggestion for improvement. Such evaluation is an essential part of each period of informal or loosely supervised activity.

Report cards constitute one of the common ways of evaluating the work of the child. *Fundamentally, they represent the teacher's report to the parent on how effective her work has been.* A word of caution is in order, however, regarding their use as evaluating devices. Many studies have shown the unreliability of grades, whether given by different people for the same work or by the same person from time to time. Further, we have considerable evidence that students from homes where school learning is not highly valued do not particularly care what grades they get. In addition, report cards are generalizations from many specific performances, difficult for the teacher to fill out fairly and difficult for the student and the parent to interpret.

The conventional report card, on which grades of A, B, C, D, and F or grades in percents are given in named subjects and perhaps in "citizenship," are still in common use because parents understand them. Such grades are quite unreliable; if a teacher should make out one set of cards, lose them and attempt to duplicate them, there would be a good deal of variation in grades given. Further, the subjects and "citizenship" itself are too complex and varied for a single grade to stand for accomplishment in that field. As a result several other ways of reporting achievement are often used in combination with modified report cards.

The modified report card differs from the conventional one in several ways. It is more specific: "Reading" becomes "Understands what he reads," "Reads rapidly," "Has an adequate vocabulary." "Citizenship" becomes "Works well with other children," "Carries through tasks he undertakes," "Shows normal poise and control," "Is ready to help others," "Shows initiative and ability to think things through for himself." Further, instead of trying to assign letter or percentage grades, there are only two or three descriptive categories. In the kindergarten or first grade, for example, there may be just one column for checking "Has shown satisfactory growth." In the primary and middle grades there may be two columns, "Has shown satisfactory growth" and "Needs help." In upper grades there may be three columns, one for "Superior," another for "Average," and the third for indicating the existence of a problem. In the newer report cards, too, the criterion on the basis of which grades are given is not the amount achieved alone, and usually not even amount achieved in relation to estimated ability, but rather the amount of progress the student has shown. In that way each individual, regardless of his pattern of abilities, has a chance to receive satisfactory grades.

On most cards, too, there is space for a comment by the teacher, and in many cases for a return comment from the parent. The free comments are sometimes the only report used. In such cases, the teacher writes a letter to the parents of each student once a semester in which she describes the work the individual has done and the progress he has made, and indicates what his needs are for future work. Such letters are more rewarding when they are carefully done, but a high level of professional competence is required to make sure that essential points are covered and the interpretation is adequately understood.

Perhaps the most practical combination of such methods is represented by the reporting-interview plan. Once each semester the teacher is given time to spend from half an hour to an hour with the parents of each student. In preparation, she prepares a folder containing samples of his work, results of standardized achievement tests, dated "anecdotal records" or notations on behavior, and perhaps a report card of some kind. She talks over with the parent what the student is accomplishing, listens to information the parent may be able to give, and makes a plan for further work on the basis of the information gained. Such informal interchange of ideas is helpful, both to parent and to teacher.

The teacher's own records of a student's work should be kept in highly specific form. Informal tests, achievement tests, anecdotal records, specimens of work, rating scales, and the like all should find their way into the folder for each individual.

In judging her own achievement of teaching goals, the teacher should be similarly specific and objective, using tests where they are pertinent, sociometric devices, situational testing, or controlled observation. The teacher, like the learner, can know when she is achieving her objectives only when she has specific pertinent knowledge on which to base that judgment.

A word of caution is in order. Knowledge of results should not become competition for scores. The effectiveness of the incentive lies in the information it gives to the learner. Knowledge of results should be informative, and not pressure to achieve more than one's classmates.

PROGRAMMED AND COMPUTER-ASSISTED INSTRUCTION

In the past decade programmed instruction has developed into a major resource for teachers. Fundamentally, much of its value lies in the careful analysis of steps in a particular field, in the learner's control of his own timing, and in immediate knowledge of whether a response is right or wrong. Carefully worked-out programs are available in a wide variety of fields.

The teacher may use such programs for an entire class or, more often, to provide individual instruction for students with specific learning needs. A fifth-grade child who has trouble with subtraction, or a geometry student who has forgotten critical parts of algebra, may be given a program which will teach him what he needs. For programmed instruction is carefully directed toward specific needs. It cannot take the place of the teacher either in determining the learner's immediate need or in over-all planning for a group. It does relieve the teacher of specific planning for many individual needs if she is aware of what is available in her field.

Neither does programmed instruction necessarily require elaborate machines for its use. Many programs are available in simple workbook form. Their value lies in sequencing, timing, and immediate feedback at each step; it is the instructional material that is important, not the mode of presentation.

Recently there has been an upsurge of research on computer-assisted instruction. Its value lies in the fact that each step presented can be modified in terms of what the learner has just done in the preceding step. It may also be quite elaborate (and expensive), as in the case of a machine for teaching young children to read: that device shows the child the word, pronounces it, has him write it on a typewriter where all but the correct key is locked each time, lets him dictate his own writing, and incorporates other features of good teaching. So far such computerized instruction, because of its cost and its highly individualized approach, is difficult to fit into the conventional school program; it is a valuable research tool because of its flexible control of variables.

IMPLICATIONS

From such studies, the following suggestions for teachers seem to emerge:

1. Adapt to the learner's natural tempo of work whenever possible. Do not urge students to hurry or to slow down. Interrupt the individual's rhythm of work for emphasis only.

2. Make scheduling of time a part of the planning for each activity. Stress quality of work as well as speed. Stress work units rather than time units.

3. Evaluate each learning experience in a suitable way. Make sure the information given is specific. Emphasize correct ways of doing things rather than mistakes. Give information on accomplishment immediately after learning. Use evaluation particularly often with bright students.

EXERCISES IN APPLICATION

1. A third-grade child has misspelled a new word in a composition. What is the best kind of correction to use? Why? Would you use the same procedure with a tenth-grade student who repeatedly misspells the same word? Why? How are the situations similar and how do they differ?

2. Suppose that a high-school history teacher gives the same test to classes of equal ability. In one he tells the students they may have thirty minutes, which is about the time most need to finish. In the other he tells them to take as long as they like. What will be the effect on the number of questions answered correctly? On each pupil's relative standing in the class? What kind of student is most likely to improve his relative position? Why?

3. Two of your instructors have assigned term papers on the same day. One said the paper is due at mid term, which is five weeks away; the other said the paper may be turned in whenever you have completed it to your satisfaction. Which paper will you turn in first? Why? What does this experience mean in your own teaching?

4. Teacher A in seventh grade makes a practice of reading critically one composition for each student each week, with detailed corrections in the margins. Teacher B grades every composition, but assigns over-all grades with general comments on the composition as a whole. Teacher C underscores the errors and turns the papers back to the students for correction. Other things being equal, in which class will the students show the greatest progress? In which the least? To what learning principles are these conclusions related?

5. How can you decide how rapidly to present a list of spelling words? Should you try to get the group to speed up through constantly accelerating your rate? What will be the effect?

6. A teacher reviewed multiplication with her fifth grade through having the children do simple problems. She said, "Let's see who can do the most

problems this time in ten minutes." Will the quality of the work done by the class improve? The quantity? What instruction could she have given that would have improved both quality and quantity?

7. Bill is a good student, but it takes him twice as long as anyone else to get his work done. What should the teacher do about it? Why?

8. Some teachers give assignments that only the bright children in the class will be able to complete, on the theory that the others will do as much as they can anyway and the bright ones must be kept busy. Analyze this practice from the point of view of the average child. Will he learn at his best level under these conditions? Why?

9. What are the major criticisms of the conventional report card? In what way does the modified report card meet these objections? With the modified report card, is the teacher-parent interview still necessary? Why?

10. The school board in city X was asked to purchase programmed instructional booklets in arithmetic fundamentals and in beginning Spanish. The board objected on the basis that teaching would be depersonalized and that costs of teaching machines would be too great. What would be your reply to the board if you were invited to a hearing on the matter?

SUGGESTIONS FOR FURTHER READING

Anderson, R. C. "Educational Psychology." *Ann. Rev. Psych., 18,* 129–164, 1967. A somewhat technical review of the psychological literature on learning, 1962–1966, including sections on instructional technology, overt response, and feedback, among others.

Atkinson, R. C. "Computerized Instruction and the Learning Process." *Amer. Psych., 23,* 225–239, 1968. A description of several modes of computer-assisted instruction, with applications to teaching reading.

Gage, N. L., ed. *Handbook of Research on Teaching,* Parts III and IV. Chicago: Rand McNally, 1963. A presentation of task and method variables in learning.

Hansen, Duncan H. "Computer Assistance with the Educational Process." *Rev. of Educ. Res., 36,* 588–603, 1966. A review of theoretical and experimental developments since 1962 that employ computer-assisted instruction.

Hendershot, C. H. *Programmed Learning: A Bibliography of Programs and Presentation Devices,* 3rd ed. San Antonio: National Society for the Study of Programmed Instruction, 1965. A bibliography of programs and presentation devices including a directory of publishers, titles, grade levels, and costs.

Lange, P. C., ed. *Programed Instruction: The Sixty-Sixth Yearbook of the National Society for the Study of Education.* Chicago: National

Society for the Study of Education, 1967. A presentation of "programed" instruction and its use in schools.

Sanford, Nevitt, ed. *The American College: A Psychological and Social Interpretation of Higher Education*, 312–363. New York: Wiley, 1962. A review of task and method variables in learning by M. J. McKeachie.

Schramm, W. *The Research on Programmed Instruction: An Annotated Bibliography*. Washington, D.C.: U.S. Department of Health, Education and Welfare, 1964. An introduction to the research and literature on programmed instruction.

Uttal, W. R. "Teaching and Machines." *Psych. Today, 1*, 20–23, 1967. A nontechnical presentation of the use of computer teaching.

Zinn, K. L. "Computer Technology for Teaching and Research on Instruction." *Rev. Educ. Res., 37*, 618–634, 1967. A review of research on computer-assisted instruction including drill, problem solving, feedback, and modification of learning materials.

Forms of Motivation: Emotional Factors

Previous chapters have indicated that motivation in the classroom falls into three groups: forms which stress understanding through information, forms which appeal directly to emotion, and forms which emphasize the child's relationship with other children. Having examined the motivational effects of information, we come to the heart of the motivational process, the procedures which set the general emotional tone of the classroom.

One of the teacher's most important functions is that of creator and maintainer of the classroom atmosphere. She must decide whether it should be an emotionless place or whether there is room for joy and celebration, whether laughter will disrupt or facilitate learning, and whether all unpleasant events or associations should be barred from the child's experience. Such issues take specific form in questions such as whether arithmetic drill should occur simply as an exercise, or whether new words in reading should be reinforced solely by repetition. Should every attempt of the child be met with "That's good," "All right," or "Fine"? What is to be said to the parent's question about whether the child should be protected from all events that adults find disturbing? Are there some instances in which his interpretation differs from theirs, and are there other cases in which gradual introduction under conditions of security will help to blunt the trauma of later experiences?

The importance of information about the affective or emotional factors in learning is perhaps evident from preceding chapters. The results of studies of propaganda show that when the same facts are presented to some subjects in the form of emotional appeal and to others in the form of reasoned argument, the emotional appeal usually causes a greater change in attitude. The studies of the effect of emotion on logical reasoning show that reasoning is influenced in the direction of preconceived conviction, as is knowledge of the truth or falsity of the conclusions. Briefly, feeling tone affects not only *whether* we learn, but also *what* we learn and *how* we learn.

The research literature falls roughly into several categories: (1) the studies of relative ease of learning and remembering when associations are pleasant, unpleasant, or indifferent; (2) the studies of free recall of experience including early childhood memories; (3) direct experimentation with positive and negative reinforcement; and (4) operant conditioning as an instructional technique. An examination of each in turn will help to clarify the facts.

MEMORY VALUE OF THE PLEASANT-UNPLEASANT-INDIFFERENT

Perhaps an initial experience with so-called **PUI** experimentation will clarify the problem. Read aloud to yourself the following words, giving about one second to each and trying to give all of them equal emphasis:

accident, adventure, air, beauty, birthday, city, compliment, debt, earthquake, explosion, family, friend, game, garbage, greed, hatred, hedge, holiday, language, laugh, level, method, murder, nausea, noon, paper, party, play, position, practice, praise, prize, process, rat, shock, sickness, sky, snake, success, suicide, table, terror, time, travel, wall

Now close your book and write as many of the words as you can recall, in any order. Then score them by placing P, U, or I after each according to the following key:

P: adventure, beauty, birthday, compliment, family, friend, game, holiday, laugh, party, play, praise, prize, success, travel
U: accident, debt, earthquake, explosion, garbage, greed, hatred, murder, nausea, rat, shock, sickness, snake, suicide, terror
I: air, city, hedge, language, level, method, noon, paper, position, practice, process, sky, table, time, wall

Count the number of P, U, and I words you recalled. The chances are that you recalled an approximately equal number of P and U words, but fewer I words. It is also probable that when you were recalling the words you felt some hesitation in writing the U words, perhaps even wondered what was wrong with you to remember so many. This experience illustrates in a simple way that we tend to inhibit using the unpleasant even if we can remember it quite clearly.

The basic design of the experiments in this area consists of selecting words of known emotional value and measuring the degree of retention for them. Perhaps the subject will be asked to list known words in three groups as you did, and to repeat all he can remember. Perhaps the degree of his emotional reaction will be registered on a galvanometer and his retention of each word then compared with its galvanometric deflection. Or, in more strictly controlled studies, nonsense words may be paired with such stimuli as odors, and learning time for the unpleasant, pleasant, and indifferent compared. Such studies have often used common words, behaviors, pictures, moods, experiences, odors, colors, and sounds.

Before attempting to summarize results from this kind of experimentation, let us go on to other kinds of studies directed toward the same end.

FREE RECALL OF EXPERIENCE

Think of the earliest incident you can remember from your own life. Be sure that it is something that you remember for yourself rather than something people in your family tell about you. Now try to place that incident in time. How old were you when it happened? Use cues such as births, deaths, places, and the like to be sure about the age. The chances are you were two or three when it occurred. Now try to classify the experience in terms of feeling tone: pleasant, unpleasant, or neutral. The chances are about equal that it will be pleasant or unpleasant; there is very little chance that it will be neutral.

A number of studies of early-childhood memories show that adults can usually consciously recall some incidents that occurred at the age of three, and that there is some evidence for less clear memories under hypnosis of events that occurred still earlier. Other investigators have analyzed remarks and accounts or recent experiences for emotional tone.

There are sources of fallacy in such studies. The relative frequency with which pleasant and unpleasant experiences occur is open to serious question; it is probable that we experience many more pleasant than unpleasant events. People also differ in their impressions of the same event; most are optimistic in outlook, interpreting more experiences as pleasant than as unpleasant. And there is some doubt as to whether the interpreted *meaning* of an experience as unpleasant at a later date is the same as the feeling tone of the experience when it occurred. Such research can only suggest possible principles; there are so many unknown variables that such hypotheses must be tested under more controlled conditions than any heretofore used.

This need for controls leads us to an exploration of a third area of research, experimental studies of positive and negative reinforcement in learning.

EXPERIMENTAL STUDIES OF POSITIVE AND NEGATIVE REINFORCEMENT

The most pertinent research of all is direct experimentation with positive and negative reinforcement. Positive reinforcement may be given verbally in the form of praise or encouragement, or nonverbally in the form of a reward such as food, money, toys, or privilege. Negative reinforcement may be given verbally as an expression of disapproval such as reproof, or nonverbally as punishment. Without trying to analyze the superstructure of theory, let us examine some of the experimentation most closely related to school situations.

The studies of verbal forms of reinforcement, specifically praise and reproof, are numerous. Laboratory experiments have included gross motor skills, peg boards, tinker toys, cancellation, jig-saw puzzles, color-naming, nonsense words and figures, and code substitution, among others. Those which have used school learning situations have been concerned with such diverse matters as spelling, arithmetic, psychological examinations, and parent-child relationships.

Now let us see whether we can bring together the results from these three types of research (memory value of the pleasant-unpleasant-indifferent; free recall of experiences; and experimental studies of positive and negative reinforcement). Some of the principles which emerge are verified in all three kinds of research; others become clear only in more carefully controlled studies.

From the studies of emotional tone in learning we can list at least twelve findings:

1. *Association with some kind of feeling tone, whether pleasant or unpleasant, aids learning and recall.* It is the emotionally colorless experience that is most difficult to remember, both immediately and later on. Both positive and negative reinforcement facilitate remembering. If a skill or attitude or other learning is to become permanent, some comment or some consequence with emotional overtones is desirable. The least favorable condition for remembering is to have an action ignored. The presence of emotion helps to isolate the learning cues. It is better for the teacher to say something than to say nothing if she wishes the child to learn from his experience.

2. *Conversely, ignoring a response helps the learner to forget it.* Sometimes the forgetting is what the teacher wants. If the student makes a mistake, whether in spelling or in playground behavior, a neutral or indifferent response or no reaction at all is the best way to avoid recurrence of acts that are not habitual. The teacher should ignore the behavior she wants the individual to forget.

3. *Negative forms of reinforcement should be used only for learnings the teacher wants the student to remember to avoid, not for those she wants him to forget.* There are occasionally dangerous acts, or fixed habits that the teacher must bring to attention in order that they be eliminated. This need applies to relatively few situations during the initial stages of learning. The learner may respond to negative reinforcement by learning not to give a punished response, or by learning to do something to avoid the school situation. The danger in using frequent or intense negative reinforcement is that the anxiety it produces is likely to generalize to related parts of the learning situations which the teacher does not want the learner to avoid; for example, too much reproof for poor handwriting may make the learner avoid all forms of written expression. Negative reinforcement generalizes more widely than positive forms.

4. *In the long run, positive forms of reinforcement facilitate learning more than negative forms.* When praise is repeated a number of times, the learning increases for an initial series of trials, then levels off; eventually the learner becomes accustomed to or dependent upon praise to maintain his own feeling of self-worth. With reprimand or failure, learning is increased immediately but falls off very soon and very rapidly; failure does not maintain its effect in stimulating learning as long or as well as praise. This

observation suggests that positive forms of reinforcement should be used in most situations.

5. *Pronounced differences in attitude occur under positive and negative forms of reinforcement.* When the child feels he is succeeding, time seems short, the task seems easy, he enjoys what he is doing, and he is more likely to resume work after interruption. When he feels that he is failing, time seems long, the task seems difficult, he dislikes what he is doing, and he is less likely to come back to the task. When he is succeeding, there is an increased activity level, greater effectiveness of work, more recall of related material, more language expression, and a longer period devoted to the initial effort. When he is failing, he becomes passive, forgets related things, and tires quickly. Children seek again those experiences in which they have succeeded and avoid those in which they have failed, but they remember both.

6. *Both positive and negative reinforcement are most effective when attached to specific acts rather than to diffuse situations.* This difference is in part due to the stronger focusing of the motivation on the behavior in question.

7. *Symbolic forms of reinforcement are effective, though nonverbal forms are more effective than verbal forms.* Actual success is superior to praise by the teacher, perhaps because the success communicates more effectively a feeling of self-worth than does a comment from an adult. Arranging situations in which the learner can succeed, and permitting him to experience the normal consequences of acts in which the teacher feels he has failed, are the most effective forms of motivation.

8. *Both positive and negative forms of reinforcement are best used immediately after or as part of the learning experience itself.* Delayed praise or reprimand, unless they are anticipated, will have relatively less effect on learning than either given immediately. An anticipated reward is about as effective as a reward given immediately, but threatened punishment is less effective than immediate negative reinforcement. The effect of the delay follows the same pattern as that for repeated use of the reinforcer; that is, the positive form maintains its effectiveness longer than the negative.

9. *Both pleasant and unpleasant feeling tone recede toward a neutral value with the passage of time.* The process of forgetting, of overlaying old experiences with new ones, operates in feeling tone as it does in more largely intellectual areas. But what we *recall* as

pleasant in meaning is sometimes different from what we *experienced* as pleasant in feeling at the time. An operation or an accident may have been unpleasant as an experience, but recalling our fortitude or heroism at the time may be highly pleasant. There is some indication that over long time intervals we avoid recalling unpleasant experiences that remain unpleasant to recall, but retain the ability to recall pleasant experiences that are pleasant to recall.

10. *Both positive and negative forms of reinforcement are best used in moderation,* and with frequent shifting in specific form. Any form loses its value if repeated often. The balance, however, should be on the positive side in the long run in order to help the child maintain his self-respect and a feeling of adequacy.

11. *Individual differences in reaction to positive and negative reinforcement are significant.* Negative forms are felt earlier than pleasant. Bright children and those whose initial standing is high can respond more constructively to negative forms than slow-learning children; the slow-learning need constant praise and they respond to rewards in a relatively greater degree than do the bright. Boys seem to be able to respond to negative forms more constructively than girls, perhaps because our culture protects girls. Older children respond to both positive and negative reinforcement more strongly than younger children, and are able to use negative forms more constructively. Praise is especially important in the preschool and primary years. Well-adjusted children have histories in which positive forms of reinforcement have predominated, while poorly adjusted children have had a higher proportion of negative reinforcement, creating insecurity. Introverts respond best to praise, particularly to continued praise; extroverts can use reprimand constructively. Some teachers, and all teachers in some situations, can use praise more effectively than reprimand; for others the situation is reversed.

12. *The child's attitude colors the result of the test.* The final assessment of the effectiveness of an incentive rests on the extent to which it has value to the particular child as a goal. We often wonder why a child finds some acts pleasant and others unpleasant. Perhaps his reaction depends upon the extent to which that act or that feeling can be integrated into his individual meaning and value system. For example, one of the factors in school failure is the socioeconomic status of the home; marks have meaning for the children from middle-class homes, but little meaning for children

from less privileged socioeconomic groups. In addition, some people seem to select an optimistic interpretation of all events, others a pessimistic one. Perhaps each selects the feeling tone that he can merge with his own frame of reference.

In general, these findings mean that emotion does have a definite place in the learning process. The teacher will admit emotion into the learning situation, and will encourage children to develop attitudes of liking and disliking and to express emotional reactions in the classroom. The classroom that confines itself to purely intellectual learning is an ineffective classroom. Emotion facilitates learning and remembering.

OPERANT CONDITIONING AS A LEARNING SYSTEM

Recently a way of learning which emphasizes positive (and sometimes negative) reinforcement has been developed, known as operant conditioning, or "behavior modification." It is based largely on the assumption that every act leading to the teaching goal should be immediately reinforced. Into the system are also built such learning conditions as careful sequencing, much formal structure, and constant knowledge of results.

To the present such techniques have been used largely and successfully with students for whom conventional classroom learning is difficult, such as the emotionally disturbed or the mentally retarded or those with specific learning difficulties. Hewett's "engineered classroom" is an illustration. The engineered classroom is structured around a hierarchy of learning tasks. Each student carries his own job card with him, and behavior appropriate to his individual goals is checked and reinforced at fifteen-minute intervals. He is given small candies for achievement, or he may choose among prizes to be given for specified numbers of checks on his work card.

Such systems simplify the use of reinforcement and other learning factors in the classroom. Thus far they seem most useful in the very early stages of learning, or with children whom the usual classroom techniques cannot reach.

REINFORCEMENT IN THE CLASSROOM

The fact that emotional values recede in time has an interesting implication. The impulse of the teacher is often to handle behavior problems immediately when they arise. The result is that the student who has been fighting, or who has been caught red-handed in stealing, or who has been rude, is still very highly motivated. When highly motivated, he responds emotionally and not rationally. By simply saying, "We'll talk about this later," and allowing a cooling-off period, the teacher as well as the student can use the conference more profitably. Then the behavior should be approached as a problem for rational analysis, with the object of clarifying what happened instead of fixing blame, and mutually deciding what should be done to right the wrong and to prevent such an error in the future. The teacher is wise to simply postpone such a conference, without threat and without punishment, knowing that in time emotion will recede and reason emerge.

In the dame school of the past, the usual form of motivation is symbolized by the bundle of switches that hung on the wall. Children learned to read, and to read well. They also learned, however, to dislike reading and to avoid it whenever they could. Today the teacher of beginning reading is aware of this fact. She uses for reading charts the words which the child already uses in talking and with which he feels secure. Words are introduced slowly and are repeated often enough that the child succeeds in mastering them easily. Picture books, stories read by the teacher, library trips, research-type reading, and free reading help to maintain a pleasurable attitude toward reading. When the child makes an error, he is given the correct word at once, and helped to remember it through drill at the end of the period. In this way children learn both to read and to like reading, and as adults they seek libraries and read freely.

By contrast the nonreader, or the student of normal intelligence with specific reading disability, carries a tremendous burden of negative attitudes. He avoids reading, and the emotional block often extends to oral and written language as well. He may become shy and withdrawn, or overaggressive, or truant. When faced with the necessity to read, he guesses wildly, repeats the same errors, or devises ways of getting others to do his reading for him. The problem of the remedial teacher is to find new ways to teach him, ways not blocked by the negative attitudes he has developed. Often this effort means teaching through different senses; sometimes in extreme cases it means learning to read in a foreign language as a starting point. It always means that reading must be attached to a strong individual interest to counteract the feeling of failure and attitude of avoidance. The teacher must ignore errors, stress correct forms, and use constant praise.

A student tutor reported an example of the importance of praise as a start towards helping one slow-learning child.

> I learned from her actions and expressions how much praise meant to her. If I said just one word of encouragement she would beam from ear to ear. I remember one time when she showed me a paper she had done in class. At the top was written, "Good, but needs a little more work." When I looked closely I saw that all she had written was her name, the title, and one word. She remarked with a smile, "The teacher thought it was good." After that she tried, though without success, to finish the work.

An illustration of negative reinforcement is found in the story of a rather shy student, studious but panic-stricken when an oral report was demanded.

> I remember very well the "current events" we used to give in class. We had been instructed to select a bit of news, phrase it carefully, and present it forcefully. Then we had to stand before the class and listen to the criticism, most of it negative, with which our efforts were greeted.
>
> The night before such an assignment was a nightmare. I would search the paper for a news item, significant but short enough to memorize easily. I went over it again and again until it recited itself, and I became a phonograph just playing it over and over again. I rehearsed on waking, and all the way to school.
>
> The report was never too good, and my terror in giving it must have been evident. At any rate, the effect of the criticism was to make any public appearance traumatic.
>
> There have been interesting products of this experience as an adult. I never volunteer for an oral report, and usually make notes before volunteering a statement in class. If I must give a speech, all the terror of the earlier experience recurs. I even have trouble memorizing anything, and wild horses could not drag me to take part in a play.

Here the difficulty was that the student was faced with a situation that meant failure to him, and the result of repeating the motivation was to make him dislike not only the giving of oral reports but also more remotely related activities.

On the other hand, consider what the teacher does to keep

interest high in beginning reading. A first-grade teacher pointed
out:

> My heart goes out to the six-year-olds struggling to make those blots of
> ink mean something. I try to make up good reading charts, related to their
> experiences, not too difficult in vocabulary, and with plenty of fun-words
> like "Whoosh!" or "Look out!" Then I let them find or draw pictures, and
> choose the right one for the chart.
>
> But even so, it is slow going for some of them. So I practically put the
> words into their mouths, and spend plenty of time reading to them. They
> love to hear stories, and to supply words just as if they were reading. I
> keep the library table full of picture books, too, so that they think of books
> as fun, and not as drudgery.

Or the effects of encouragement may be even more far-reaching,
as a student in training for teaching pointed out:

> I came from a home in which no English was spoken, and my halting
> attempts to speak and read and write were confusing and even irritating to
> most of my teachers. I used to cry every day on the way home from school,
> and wonder how long they would let such an unintelligent child stay
> there.
>
> In the fourth grade, though, I found a teacher who was different. She
> would correct my pronunciation, then praise my attempt to say the word
> correctly. She found easy books especially for me, and suggested I read
> them to the younger children at home. She had me tell the class about the
> people of my own native background, something that none of the rest of
> them could do.
>
> I not only learned much about English and reading, but I learned what
> a teacher can really mean to a child. It was because of her that I decided to
> become a teacher myself, to help other children who need encouragement
> in order to learn things that are difficult for them.

In teaching in the content fields such as social studies, the same
principles operate. The teacher plans an exhibit of pictures or an
excursion or a visit from a resource person as a starting point for a
new interest. After group discussion, each child finds a related task
at which he can work successfully, proceeds with the commendation
and criticism of the class as a guide, and develops a lasting interest
as he learns. Negative feeling is avoided so that energy may be
released and favorable attitudes created.

In the arts, appreciation is built on positive reinforcement. The
child is given materials which are easy to control so that he may be

reasonably successful in his work. Crayons and poster paints precede work with water colors. The good qualities in his attempts are pointed out, and positive suggestions for improvement are made. Here attitude is a major objective.

With so much stress on positive criticism and avoidance of emphasis on error, the impression may arise that negative reinforcement should never be used. That impression is wrong; negative reinforcement is useful in blocking objectionable acts. The function of negative emotional tone is to block an existing behavior, or to check behavior that is dangerous or so firmly fixed that it stands in the way of substituting an acceptable pattern. "No" has a legitimate place. Suppose the child wants to play with the knobs on the stove, thus turning on the gas? Or to run after his ball in a crowded street? Or to open the door of the car while it is still in motion? Quick, decisive, negative action is needed. Two of these situations were described by a parent, who showed the legitimate use of negative action:

My little girl liked to play in the kitchen while I was working, to do everything I did. Of course that sometimes brought trouble. She wanted to play at the stove, and was hard to discourage. I tried showing her that turning the knob was something that Mommy must always do. She tried it again, and in desperation I simply shouted, "No!" She was startled, but I picked her up and put her down in front of a cupboard full of kettles. I showed her how to open the door by turning the knob, and when she tired of that she became absorbed in the beautiful noises the kettles made when she brought them out and stacked them. I had to watch her for a while, but soon she went to the cupboard instead of the stove.

We had a similar problem with her older brother. He loved to play with the handle of the door on the car. We tried tying it shut, but he was ingenious in loosening it. A strong "No" from his Dad stopped him for only a little while. We hastily decided it would be better to let him bring his dog along to keep him busy during such trips, and when we finally stopped we showed him how to untie and open the door. After a little watching, he remembered that doors were to be opened only when the car was standing still.

When a young child throws sand at another, the parent checks the behavior by diverting the energy thus blocked into some form of active play. When a child destroys a pueblo the class has built, the teacher lets the class show its feeling toward him, then follows immediately by giving him some plan for restitution.

In the case of a well-developed habit in an adult, even negative practice may be of value provided the learner practices always with the thought that he is practicing an *error*. For example, a typist who frequently writes *hte* for *the* may eliminate the faulty habit by writing lines of *hte* and thinking "This is *wrong*" until she is very tired of writing it. Such methods are appropriate only for wrong habits that are firmly fixed, not for right habits in the initial stages of formation. Even though negative practice is sometimes useful in breaking wrong habits, it does not automatically establish correct patterns. It only blocks the wrong behavior in preparation for the establishment of right responses.

In dealing with most problem behavior in children the best procedure is to avoid emphasis or emotional tone. Young children often pick up expletives or expressions at home or on the school ground that have little meaning for them other than that they cause excitement. One teacher, for example, found a child of ten distributing to her classmates a set of playing cards backed with pictures of pin-up girls.

I had visions of what would happen if all the children took those cards home and showed them to their parents. So I asked the child who had done the distributing where she got them. She said they were her parents' favorite cards, they liked the pictures, and maybe her friends would, too. Questioning brought out the fact, however, that her parents did not know she had brought the cards to school.

It didn't seem worthwhile to go into the whole question of why adults would think her a bad girl for doing this. So I just secured her agreement that her parents would miss the cards and feel sorry they were gone (and left it to her to imagine the action her parents would take toward her if they found out). Then I helped her collect them as quietly as possible, check to see that she had a complete pack, and kept them until time for her to take them home.

A child who uses obscene language often does not know its meaning for adults: ignoring his behavior will help him to forget, whereas punishing him will help him to remember what he said. He needs to learn to substitute a few socially acceptable shock words or expletives. When he seems to be impertinent, he is often only sincere and direct; answering him and including in the answer a suggestion on how his thought might have been phrased will turn him to more acceptable forms. We tend too often to bring up the big guns against acts which for children have meanings quite different from those they have for adults. If a teacher ignores the error, the child will forget it more easily and will more quickly learn the correct form of behavior that is substituted.

Sometimes, of course, children engage in shock behavior simply because unfavorable attention is better than no attention at all, or because it makes them feel grown-up. A junior-high-school principal one day arrived at work a little earlier than usual.

I found one of the smallest, most inconspicuous members of the seventh-grade class standing just behind the pine tree at the main entrance, apparently puffing on a corn-cob pipe. I asked him to come into the building with me.

After a few preliminary activities, enough for me to figure that one out, I explained to him that smoking was harmful to boys and forbidden on the school grounds by state law. "I know," he said. "But this isn't tobacco; it is pine needles," and he showed me his pouch.

"Just the same," I said, "I think you would give the wrong impression by having those things on you. Don't you want me to keep them for you until you are ready to go home?"

"Aren't you going to call my father?" he asked, more in disappointment than astonishment. I assured him I was not, but said, "Since you are here early, I do need some help in the store room putting the athletic supplies in order. Would you have time to work at it?" Of course he would, and we kept up a desultory conversation through the adjoining room until time for school.

He couldn't quite part with his shock material until after school, however. He came in at afternoon recess and asked whether he could have it. "Are you sure you can keep it out of sight until you get home, not show it to any one, not even tell them about it?" He was. So I gave it to him, and as far as I know he kept his part of the bargain.

Even when the behavior is intended to shock, it is often best to meet it with as little attention as possible, and to supply in some socially acceptable form the attention it was intended to gain.

STUDIES OF FAILURE AND ITS EFFECTS

In addition to the comparative studies of positive and negative reinforcement, there have been a number of specific studies of the effect of failure itself. They are particularly important since there is increasing doubt that success and failure constitute extremes on the same continuum. The effect of success seems to be to reinforce the response or habit or attitude. The effect of failure is diverse; under some conditions it causes frustration and aggression, and under others regression and withdrawal.

Laboratory studies have investigated many aspects of success and failure. There have also been a number of studies of "failure" as it is defined in schools, that is, as repetition of grade. Most studies of grade repetition have been concerned with the causes of nonpromotion, though some have gone on to study the effect of nonpromotion on subsequent learning and have examined alternatives to nonpromotion.

Studies of the effect of failure seem to show that failure is not comparable to success in the sense of being its opposite but that instead, the effects of failure differ in quality. Specifically:

1. *Failure depresses the action potential.* Muscular action normally accompanies attempted solution of problems. There is usually a decreased motility level under failure. Sometimes there is speeding up to relieve tension at the expense of efficiency of work. Sometimes "sparking-over" to activities not directed to learning occurs.

2. *Failure slows learning.* It decreases the number of correct responses and increases the time taken to give them. It results in apathy or depressed psychological functioning as a defense against complete awareness of failure. It means a decreased sensitivity to potentially disturbing stimuli, both internal and external.

3. *Failure causes a moving away from reality.* Quitting, daydreaming, and regression are common. Social responsiveness is reduced. Work is dogged and ineffectual. The task also is decontextualized, or split off from its social frame of reference.

4. *Failure causes persistent nonadjustive behavior,* and tends to fix incorrect response patterns. Frequent punishment of the wrong response is more likely to cause the response to occur again than to eliminate it. This response is especially probable if the child knows he is wrong but does not know what is right. Reprimand also strengthens the response by serving as an informative signal.

5. *Failure increases the variability of behavior.* Some children show aggression, others regression, some respond with skepticism and some with panic. Some do the same thing over and over mechanically; others "freeze." The effect of failure seems to be to intensify whatever response pattern is dominant in the child at the

moment. Individual differences increase under failure, decrease with success.

6. *The effect of failure is cumulative.* We have already noted that repeated failure is damaging, and that anticipated failure interferes with learning. There is greater danger of over-motivation and disruption of learning in failure than in success.

7. *Failure causes changes in attitudes as well as in ability to remember.* It shortens the child's time perspective, makes him think of the minutes spent in learning as long, of the learning as difficult and unpleasant. It makes him forget related material he previously knew. The relation of these facts to nonpromotion is of interest.

8. *Training can correct these ineffective behaviors by introducing progressively more difficult tasks in which the child succeeds.* With success comes interest, self-direction, and elimination of nonadjustive behavior. For example, trial promotions result in as much learning as nonpromotions, and grades in new subjects tend to be higher than those in repeated subjects.

. . . IN THE CLASSROOM

We have seen that learning is made more difficult by the occurrence of failure. It is best, of course, to make it possible for the student to succeed initially; then there is no problem in learning or in interest. When initial failure occurs, the best thing for the teacher to do is to shift to some other learning without letting the learner feel his failure too keenly, then to come back to the original learning in some new form at another time and make sure of success then. The teacher who emphasizes the failure establishes a block to learning that gets in the way of learning the correct response later. To prevent such blocks, children who are not ready to read are not exposed to too strong motivation or forced to read early; the teacher, by simply letting them watch the other children and join in when they wish, but not forcing them to learn words, makes it possible for them to learn to read more easily at some time in the future. To insist on reading makes it inevitable that the unready child will fail, and creates emotional blocking and disinterest which will hinder the work of the future teachers who will take over the problem of teaching him reading.

Similarly, the learner should be protected from any situation in which he is foredoomed to failure because of limited ability. The outmoded traditional spelling match is an illustration. In that situation, the poor speller went down first, in public disgrace, and tried his best to protect his ego by not listening while the good spellers were praised. The effect was to intensify his difficulty with spelling. Instead, one training supervisor suggests:

> Let them have their spelling matches, but make them profitable for everybody. Instead of having a student sit down when he misses a word, just put down a tally on the board each time a team gets a word right. Instead of giving everybody words of equal difficulty, give each student a word you think he has a good chance of being able to spell. Instead of having the words spelled orally, have the teams rotate to the board and write the words. That way it is still a game, has value as drill on spelling in the way in which spelling is used, and protects the ego of everyone.

When errors are pointed out, the pointing should be done with a maximum of ego support for the child in order to help him accept the criticism and use the information profitably. Education is in a sense built on frustrating some actions and rewarding others, so the child should be helped to constructively meet normal frustrations. This help must come slowly and by small degrees, however. Reprimand before others or public correction of mistakes is more damaging than is speaking to a child privately. Such criticism as is given should follow the formula of finding something good to say, pointing out the problem, and suggesting what to do, so that the balance of the criticism is positive. Whenever there is negative criticism the teacher should open up some form of compensatory outlet in which the individual can succeed.

The decision regarding whether to promote a student is an important one. A counselor, working with the problem in one school district, found:

> Teachers tend to overemphasize such things as regular attendance, unobtrusive and "good" behavior, and obvious "effort" in making their decisions. They think of what the child has done during the past year, and not the broad complex of factors that make him achieve.
>
> They need to re-orient their thinking. In deciding whether a child should repeat a grade, the one question is, "Will the conditions for learning be better if he stays with me in this grade than they will if he goes on to another teacher with his class?" If he is a bright child who has missed school, he will be able to make up the work quickly and repetition would damage his social adjustment. If the repetition would place him in a class with a younger sibling, the same thing may be true. If he is slow in

learning, plays with younger children, and lacks confidence, perhaps retention would be a good idea. But in any case a grade should always be repeated with a *different* teacher. If a child failed once with the procedures one teacher uses, he is likely to fail again, and he has in addition the carry-over effect of having failed. If he is to have a chance to succeed, he needs a complete change of school environment.

It is usually well to check any decision about repetition of grade with the school counselor or principal. It is often advisable to test the decision by trial promotion for a limited period of time as well. Many children do surprisingly well when given a chance.

IMPLICATIONS

From these studies, the following implications for teachers seem to emerge:

1. Introduce feeling tone only into activities that you wish the learner to remember. Ignore behavior you wish him to forget. Delay handling strongly emotional problems until the child involved has recovered his poise.

2. Use negative reinforcement only in activities you wish the learner to remember, dislike, and avoid. Keep negative feeling tone moderate at all times. Follow negative reinforcement by positive suggestion.

3. Use positive reinforcement in activities you wish the learner to remember and repeat. Keep the balance of feeling positive for each individual. Arrange situations in which the student can succeed in preference to depending on praise. Vary the feeling tone from time to time.

4. Select the form of reinforcement that is best for the particular individual. Use positive forms more often with young children, girls, the slow-learning, the maladjusted, and the introverted. Use negative forms somewhat more freely with older children, boys, the rapid-learning, well-adjusted, and extroverted.

EXERCISES IN APPLICATION

1. How can you distinguish between the kinds of misbehavior for which the teacher should use negative reinforcement and those which she should ignore? Give an illustration of each.

2. Liza is a fourth grader with difficulty in word recognition. Her teacher gave her an assignment, and asked her to reread it until she could read it perfectly. She has tried and failed to read it correctly to her teacher

three times. What is likely to be her performance on the fourth trial? Why?

4. Do the effects of success or failure increase or decrease in degree with repetition? What does the answer mean for the teacher's handling of failure situations?

5. In retelling an event that was fundamentally unpleasant, why do we tend to retell more of the pleasant side than the unpleasant? What does this tendency mean about the nature of memory for the pleasant? What other factors affect the situation?

6. In free recall of experience, the chances are about equal that you will recall what type of incident over a neutral one? Why?

7. What would be a teacher's action if she wants a child to forget something? To avoid it in the future? Why do the two situations differ?

8. Is actual success more desirable as reinforcement than praise by the teacher? Which is more effective—threatened punishment or negative result? Promised reward or immediate reward? Why?

9. What is the relationship between emotional stability and positive and negative reinforcement? As a determiner of nature of reaction? As a result of frequent use of the form of reinforcement?

10. What are some of the practices a teacher might well take over from operant conditioning? With what kinds of learners and what kinds of learning will they be most successful?

SUGGESTIONS FOR FURTHER READING

Allen, S. A. "The Effects of Verbal Reinforcement on Children's Performance as a Function of Type of Task." *J. Exptl. Child. Psych., 3*, 57–73, 1966. A study of the use of praise, criticism, and silence in teaching children.

Blough, D. S., and R. B. Millward. "Learning: Operant Conditioning and Verbal Learning." *Ann. Rev. Psych., 16*, 63–94, 1965. A somewhat technical review of the psychological literature on operant conditioning, reinforcement, timing, and rote learning.

Franks, C. M., and Dorothy J. Susskind. "Behavior Modification with Children: Rationale and Technique." *J. Sch. Psych., 6*, 75–88, 1968. A description of the background of the behavior-modification approach and of its use with children.

Hewett, M. F. *The Emotionally Disturbed Child in the Classroom: A Developmental Strategy for Educating Children with Maladaptive Behavior.* Boston: Allyn and Bacon, 1968. A presentation of the "engineered classroom" for emotionally disturbed children, based on a developmental sequence of educational goals.

Krumboltz, J. D. "Meaningful Learning and Retention: Practice and Reinforcement Variables." *Rev. Educ. Res., 31*, 535–546, 1961. A summary of research on reinforcement, positive and negative, touching on learner activity and knowledge of results as well as on emotional factors.

Lewis, D. J. "Partial Reinforcement: A Selective Review of the Literature since 1950." *Psych. Bull.*, *57*, 1–28, 1960. A review of studies of the effects of partial reinforcement on learning and forgetting.

Skinner, B. F. *The Technology of Teaching*. New York: Appleton-Century-Crofts, 1968. A group of Skinner's speeches and papers on learning in relation to the technology of teaching.

Symonds, P. M. "What Education Has to Learn from Psychology." *Teach. Coll. Rec.*, *57*, 15–25 and 449–462, 1955–1956. An analysis of psychological literature pertinent to teaching, with emphasis on reward and punishment.

Ullman, L. P., and L. Krasner. *Case Studies in Behavior Modification*. New York: Holt, 1965. A presentation of behavior modification with special sections on children and on the mentally retarded.

Walker, E. L. *Conditioning and Instrumental Learning*. Belmont: Brooks-Cole, 1967. A survey of theory and research on operant conditioning, reinforcement vs. contiguity, transfer, and mathematical models.

Forms of Motivation: Social Factors

Much of the learner's motivation comes from the other students with whom he works. The teacher has to decide when to use group work and when to use individual study, and how to set up the right kind of group for the most effective work. Let us examine the kinds of social stimulation the individual may feel, and how he will respond.

The pressures of membership in any group constantly vary. It is difficult to eliminate hidden group pressures, or to single out certain of them for study. We know that the individual's inner aloneness is different from that which may seem to be imposed by the conditions under which he works. Even in isolation the cultural norms of behavior which he has internalized are still operative. Clearly education takes place in a group situation, and the group must always be reckoned with in studying individual actions.

There are a number of different kinds of studies of social factors in motivation. Some are concerned with social facilitation, that is, with whether the mere presence of others doing similar work affects what the learner does. Others are studies of audience effects, pertinent in the classroom because whenever other students can overhear him the individual has an audience and his behavior is changed thereby. There are studies of competition, its origins, and its effects. There are studies of cooperation which show the conditions under which people work together effectively. There are studies of the effectiveness of group work and of group judgment. The studies come not only from the psychologists; anthropologists and sociologists also are vitally interested in the same problems. And modern educational philosophy presents points of view closely interwoven with these areas.

SOCIAL FACILITATION

Let us begin with the question whether any child, old enough to have become accustomed to interaction with other people, will learn as well or less well with others present. The research question is whether the mere presence of other people in the same room, doing the same thing, not watching or competing with or helping the learner, will affect the learning. Although it is difficult under such circumstances to eliminate self-imposed competition, it is kept to a minimum. The attempt is to determine whether the mere sight and sound of others doing the same thing facilitates learning. The teacher meets this question in trying to decide whether it would be best to individualize instruction; the parent meets it in choosing between a tutorial type of education and group instruction; and the community as a whole meets it in the claims that radio and television might substitute for the classroom in the future.

Fundamentally, such research has been directed toward whether work done in the presence of one or more others is superior to work done alone, either in effectiveness or in the attractiveness of the task. Such studies seem to show that:

1. *Working in a group stimulates individual output.* This stimulation occurs whether or not there is interaction between members of the group, though it is intensified with interaction. The learner shows greater speed, though the work tends to be of the same quality as that done alone. There is a heightened activity level, and perhaps an unconscious competitive attitude. The increase is greater in routine tasks, though it is present to some extent in such activities as problem solving.

How well an individual performs in a group is related to his status, both actual and as he perceives it. If he is high in rank, or if his teacher makes him feel he has status, he will perform better. Social responses from teacher or classmates, even nodding the head or saying "Mmm" or listening attentively, can improve individual output, especially when the student has had little prior attention.

2. *Attitudes toward work done under social stimulation are more favorable than attitudes toward work done alone.* When a learner has worked with others on a task, he is more likely to continue to work on it when he is alone. When a classmate is introduced the learner may be drawn back to a task of which he has tired.

3. *Variability increases in the social stituation.* Social stimulation brings out the behaviors discussed previously as evidences of heightened motivation. Since social facilitation is mild, its effect is that of increasing the rate of activity.

4. *Learners differ in the extent to which they are affected by social facilitation.* Children under three are relatively unconscious of the presence of other children, hence show little social facilitation. Students of average mental ability show more social facilitation than very bright children; in fact, the bright child does his best work alone, especially on relatively difficult tasks.

Some authors have suggested that individuals behave in different ways when they are in a group and when they are alone. This difference is particularly marked in an interacting group. Merging oneself in a group results in a submerging of the self, a process of "de-individuation" in which one attends to the group as a group but not to the individuals in the group as individuals. Any one person, then, does not feel singled out in any action of another individual. Similarly, the inner restraints which had prohibited some forms of behavior when a person was alone are released to the group, which then may bring about new behaviors by its sanction. Much of this theoretical material is more pertinent to the co-working group (below) than to social facilitation, though it has a bearing on both.

. . . IN THE CLASSROOM

The research, then, demonstrates an advantage in teaching children in groups in a face-to-face situation. In these days of radio and television, we sometimes lose sight of this fact. There is more to learning than mastering particular facts or skills, and even the learning of skills is more fun if there are others learning with us. Students are motivated by the mere presence of others.

Both teachers and parents use this fact. Asking a child to help mother polish the bathtub or do the dishes is a much surer way to enlist his aid than asking him to do such things alone. Asking two students to work together on a task will make that task more attractive. The mere presence of others doing the same thing adds to the strength of the motivation.

Fundamentally, a teacher who decided to try to build motivation for reading through dramatization was using social facilitation as an incentive.

I was having a great deal of difficulty in holding the interest level in reading high during the last two weeks of school. Reading was hard for this group, and the distractions of an approaching vacation were great.

Rummaging around in the school library I found several copies of a book of plays. I knew my class enjoyed dramatization, so I took out the set to try it out. I asked one small group to choose a play for the class to present, but found they were taking a great deal of time, though working with great absorption. Investigation showed that, instead of choosing a play, they were assigning parts among themselves and reading the whole book of plays. That set of books certainly saw hard use by the time everyone in class had a turn at that kind of reading.

College students sometimes use essentially the same form of motivation in getting down to work when the going is hard. If there is an examination pending, going to the library where everyone else is studying and there is little to do except study may help in getting down to work. Or joining a group that is talking about a term paper that ought to be already under way may help in getting the research going. Merely associating with other people who are doing a given thing suggests that we, too, should join in the activity.

AUDIENCE EFFECTS

If the audience situation in the average classroom is assumed to be the student reciting aloud or otherwise performing as the center of attention, we miss the full impact of audience effect. Most of the things done at school are done before others. The mere presence of others leads to anticipation of an audience and its effects; at one time or another we all feel eyes upon us when we are in the presence of others, even though we are not actually the center of attention at that moment. The impassive faces of a potential audience may even constitute a threat to the insecure individual.

The effect of an audience on the learner, as an aspect of social motivation in learning, has yet to be explored experimentally to any significant degree. There have been studies of performance alone compared with performance before an audience. Most of them are concerned with the nature of the audience, whether large or small, quiet or responsive, attentive or inattentive.

Summarizing the results from the various sources, we find:

1. *The presence of an audience increases speed in performance.* There is a stepping up of the activity level and an increase in the intensity of work. This is the result of the need to be well thought of by others; the student becomes more ego-involved, and can tolerate less frustration. The audience effect wears off fairly soon, however.

2. *The presence of an audience does not improve the quality of work done.* This experience is especially true with difficult problems. The work done in a group remains the same in quality, or deteriorates. This effect applies especially to retention. Learning is retained longer when no audience is present.

3. *The known audience is less disturbing than the unknown audience.* There is some evidence that a large audience affects performance more than a small one, and an attentive audience more than an inattentive one. An unseen audience is more disturbing than one seen; people "out there" watching and listening but unseen and hence not available for evaluation by the performer are more threatening than is an audience open to observation. Similarly, introducing an unanticipated audience disturbs performance.

4. *Serving as one's own audience is disturbing.* This is the situation in which the learner's voice is recorded and played back, or when any objective means of reflecting performance is employed. There is some evidence of temporary speech and personality disorganization under such circumstances. The learner stimulates himself as well as the audience while performing, and he constantly monitors his own behavior.

5. *Observing others before an audience improves performance.* Seeing someone else's behavior before an audience, thus vicariously sharing the reinforcement he receives, leads to learning on the part of the member of the audience.

6. *Individual differences are important.* Older students are more conscious of the audience than younger, hence audience effects on the older are more pronounced. This difference is consistent with what we know of children's social development. The initially poor achiever or slow learner is helped somewhat by the presence of the audience, but the high achiever or the bright child is quite likely to

be disturbed by it. The reason may be that bright students are mentally older and more sensitive to stimulation of all forms. Audience effects should be handled particularly carefully with older and more able students.

Perhaps the best generalization from the inadequate evidence is that saying anything to the learner before others intensifies whatever motivation or feeling the indvidual already has. The audience creates no new direction in motivation but steps up the force of the existing feeling. When an audience is introduced, it should be used chiefly for accenting positive feelings. The learner should know its nature and composition in order to have time to adapt to the situation.

. . . IN THE CLASSROOM

To give the learner knowledge of his status before the class is to emphasize the importance of that status; the mere statement that his problem has been correctly solved gains force when made before others. To praise or to reprimand a student before a group, or to arrange a success situation before a group, is to increase the feeling tone attached to that situation. When interest is lagging badly, or when the learner especially needs reassurance, the teacher may wish to praise him or to help him succeed before his classmates. The teacher who asks an individual to show his picture to the class or to serve as class secretary at the blackboard is making use of this principle.

One science teacher told how she was able to help a very shy boy.

I had watched him for several days. He sat near the back of the room. He never spoke, and seemed embarrassed if he was asked a question. I didn't dare try any direct approach because of his extreme shyness.

On my way home from school, however, I had seen him working with his father around their hives of bees. That gave me an idea. When we came to the unit on insects and their habits I turned some of the questions in his direction. He answered at first in few words, but eventually he offered to bring in a hive and explain the process of making and extracting honey. He did a good job, and the class was appreciative.

From that point on, there was no problem. I could have praised him and talked with him, but that would not have helped him overcome his shyness in relation to other students. Their warm and sincere appreciation of his skill in this field did what I could not have done alone.

The problem of oral reports in the upper grades is closely related. Students forget their reports regularly, or perhaps freeze or engage in clowning instead of doing more serious work. In such a case the audience situation has been too stimulating, and has overshadowed interest in content.

The chief danger in using the class as audience lies in the possibility of over-motivation. Incentives are usually most effective used in moderate amounts. To strengthen the emotional factor too much may disrupt learning. For example, a counselor relates:

A teacher in a seventh-grade class made a practice of reprimanding before the whole class any student who failed to do his homework. One boy, accustomed to being in some kind of difficulty or other with his teacher, covered his embarrassment by making witty remarks, clowning, and in general getting the sympathy of the class. A shy girl used every opportunity to avoid class by pretending to be sick.

The most serious effect, however, was on a sensitive girl who always had her assignments done but who, because of what she saw happening to the others, was afraid she might be the next for public rebuke. She cried often, spent much too much time on making her homework mechanically perfect, and managed to complete the course only because she was supported emotionally by another teacher.

It is the effect on the observer that constitutes one of the most serious hazards in using public reprimand. Because of the danger of over-motivation, reprimand should seldom be used in the presence of others.

It is also true that the learner should face the type of social situation anticipated for his ultimate use of the material. Here the logic is similar to that suggested in handling distractions. He should learn to handle the normal level of social attention for each situation. For example, he should learn to handle being a member of a musical group or taking part in a class play so that he will not be over-motivated in such situations as an adult. There is no need, however, for him to become accustomed to social attention in arithmetic or spelling.

Sometimes, with a very withdrawn student, the teacher must simply wait until he shows interest, since he may feel any show of attention or concern as an attack. He may need to simply sit in his own emotional corner for a time until he feels quite safe in having people around him. When he begins to show an interest in others and in moving about, the teacher can unobtrusively offer help. This kind of behavior is normal in very young children and the handling of it is illustrated by a wise mother of a child who was approaching two.

We were going to leave our little girl with strangers for the day, and we knew how traumatic the adjustment to new people might be. Fortunately, when we took her into the strange house the hosts did not give her too much attention. She clung to me, wanted to sit in my lap, and looked about the room slowly. We adults talked.

After a little while she relaxed. They offered her some boxes which she fitted together, then some pans that made noises. She slipped to the floor and began trying to stack them.

Then one of the adults went to the piano and struck a note. Her attention was attracted, and soon she went over to the piano to observe better. Then, and only then, was she willing for the stranger to pick her up and talk with her. I soon slipped out, with never a tear on her part.

If a student is particularly sensitive to an audience there are a number of things the teacher can do. She can read his story for him at first, later allow him to read seated at his own desk, perhaps later ask him to come to the front of the room so that others can hear better. She can let him turn in written reports instead of making oral ones for awhile. She can encourage his joining a chorus or serving as prompter for a play, gradually shifting to a part he plays alone and on stage. The important thing is not to force an increase in attention until he knows the situation well and the intensity of his feeling has decreased a little.

COMPETITION

Competition is important in our society. In every area of the business world, in sports, and to some degree in education, individual attainment is emphasized. As a result, group and individual rivalry are powerful incentives in stimulating pupils to work at their maximum performance. They also drive children at times to cheat and chisel and bluff.

Here we come to the dilemma in which education often finds itself when philosophy and science seem to lead in different directions. Educational philosophers say that, in order to survive in a world as interdependent and as small as ours, we must learn how to work with others, both individually and as groups. We assume then, that competition should be stressed less than it is in our culture.

Psychologists tell us that competition is a strong form of motivation, especially for those who can do good work. To say that competition is ineffective would be wrong. The teacher wonders, then, whether failing to use competition is unrealistic and ineffective.

Anthropologists and sociologists tell us that we are a highly competitive people. They show the gradation from competitiveness to cooperativeness in primitive peoples, then analyze our own culture and find in it much individualism and striving to excel. They conclude that children are competitive because our culture teaches them to be competitive through its many nuances and attitudes. If we stop stressing competition we are changing our culture.

But let us examine the whole area of competition from the psychological point of view and see what the facts are. There have been many studies using animals; they compete whenever another individual interferes with attaining a goal. The development seems to be from attack on one-who-interferes or barrier behavior, to competition, to dominance, to peck-order or hierarchies in which certain individuals have privileges based on seniority or position, to the teaching of competition as we find it in our society. Though competition is largely a product of social development, it appears almost universally in human societies and to a large degree in animal groups. The particular form of competition, its intensity, and the objects over which it will occur depend largely on the degree of socialization of the individual and on the society of which he is a part.

Research specifically with human beings has produced a number of studies of competition itself, as distinguished from studies of social facilitation and studies comparing competition and cooperation.

From these studies we find that:

1. *Competition increases the amount of work done, but quality remains the same or deteriorates.* There is improvement with competition in simple mechanical tasks, but work on more difficult tasks is inhibited.

2. *The more personal the competition, the greater its effect.* Children prefer competition against their own records, and work under such conditions is as good as that done in competition against others. For older students, competition against another individual is superior to competition against a group.

3. *For the learner to be motivated, he must think he has a good chance of success in competition.* When he thinks he has no chance of winning, either because he has usually failed or because he knows his competitor is a champion, his attitude causes failure behavior. There is inhibition of overt response, lack of confidence, and physical tension growing out of the deflection of energy from thinking to feeling. Giving the learner a handicap based on his previous record, however, permits him to feel that he might succeed, and increases the sureness of his learning and the energy he puts into the task.

4. *Older students respond more to competition than do younger children.* The reason is the increasing social awareness that comes with age, combined with the home and school pressures that foster competitive attitudes. The critical period for the emergence of competition is from ages four to six. By the time the child enters the elementary school he is already responding to competitive stimuli, both these specifically imposed and those implicit in our culture.

5. *Average or slow learners repond more favorably to competition than do rapid ones.* Competition inhibits the performance of the rapid learner; he is more likely to have and respond to intrinsic or internalized standards while the average student develops internalized standards more slowly and hence is more influenced by socially imposed demands. The rapid learner is more likely to think for himself and have highly individual interests, goals, and conduct norms; the average student is more likely to be responsive primarily to social demands. The pressure of the culture is always toward conformity to the average in behavior. The less able learner has an upward pressure operating, one which raises his performance in relation to the social group; the more able learner feels a downward pressure from the same stimulation, a pressure that scales his performance toward the average even though his own way of doing things may be better. The pressure of social forms of motivation is a leveling one, in which the more able learner gains less than the others.

In addition, the bright student is more perceptive of the pressures in his environment, so that any pressure may easily become overmotivation for him. It is important to remember that the chief gain in competition lies in speed of performance, with no gain in quality of work. It is in quality of work that the rapid learner needs stimulation and responds favorably.

These findings indicate that competition is a highly effective form of motivation, particularly in increasing the rate of work. To deny its effectiveness is to deny the evidence, theoretical objections notwithstanding. However, competition is best used in the form of self-competition and in situations where every person has a real chance for success.

. . . IN THE CLASSROOM

In teaching arithmetic or spelling the teacher may encourage children to keep their own charts and to try to excel their previous scores from day to day. Some reading drill books have norms against which the child may compete. Many games and competitions can be modified by the thoughtful and inventive teacher so that self-competition occurs.

Competitive sports have evolved several devices that can minimize the harmful effects of competition. In individual competition, the person is often given a handicap based on his previous record so that he may have some chance of winning; thus he is competing with his own record as well as with his adversary. In both individual and group sports, participants are often classed according to size or weight or age so that they are fairly evenly matched. In group sports, although winning the game is important, the counterbalancing effect of supporting the other members of the team takes the edge off the competitive motive. Using competitive games between small groups which vary in membership is stressed increasingly, and competition between schools is less emphasized. Even in sports, competition is being modified to avoid individual disappointment and long-term rivalry.

So much for competition. It is effective in our culture.

COOPERATION

The anthropologists say, however, that competition is effective only because we live in a competitive culture, and that cultures differ in this respect. The competitiveness of a culture depends, not on its subsistence level or the degree of technical development, but on the social concept of success. The competitive society is characterized by a social structure depending on individual initiative, valuation of property for individual ends, a single scale of success, and strong ego development. The cooperative society is characterized by a social structure giving a high degree of security for the individual, placing weak emphasis on rising status and initiative, and stressing faith in an ordered universe. Whether a given individual responds to competition depends upon whether he was born into a competitive society.

In the United States we are highly competitive. Witness these aspects of our culture: (1) we believe in the future rather than in the past and are always changing and readjusting for that reason; (2) we are willing to scrap anything that is old; (3) we are still groping for a pattern that will give a highly diverse people a sense of belonging; (4) we believe in success, are all climbers, and expect children to excel their parents; (5) we need to believe choice and initiative are ours if we are to live with satisfaction in such a culture; and (6) we must always believe we are right because ours is a culture full of moral judgments of good and bad. All the consequent pressures, developing because of our newness and diverse origins and the ever-present frontier, have produced much individualism in the United States.

The anthropologists say, then, that the findings of psychologists concerning the strength of competitive motivation indicate only that we teach children to compete rather than to cooperate. Such training comes, in part, through the child's observation of adult behavior with its stress on keeping up with the Joneses and on success defined in terms of money and material things. The home adds to competitiveness through comparisons between the child and others: he does not handle his table manners as well as his brother, or keep as clean as the boy next door, or get grades as good as those his father got. Schools teach competitiveness in all these ways, and in addition they hold contests which cause insecurity in the classroom.

Here the educational philosopher enters the argument. He says competition is effective; it is effective because we are a competitive culture; but if we are to survive our culture must become less competitive and more cooperative. The arguments range from our increased interdependence on each other for food and shelter and clothing in an industrialized society to the fact that modern transportation makes distant and highly different cultures our next-door neighbors, requiring peaceful and helpful social interaction in the world that is emerging. The philosopher claims that the school must not only mirror the society that exists, but also anticipate the society which will exist when the children now in school are adults.

The question becomes, then, not simply one of what is the most effective form of social motivation in our society now, but one of what skills the child will need in the society of twenty years hence. For this reason, the philosopher says, we should use in schools only those forms of competition that do not interfere with the development of good interpersonal relationships and of a social conscience.

The problem is interesting as an illustration of the dilemma in which the teacher sometimes finds herself, torn between a philosophical point of view and a scientific fact. The pressure is to accept one and deny the other. Actually, the two are complementary and equally essential. Philosophy determines values and directions; it sets the goal the teacher wishes to accomplish. Science describes the behavior that will occur when the teacher does certain things, and what can be done to modify that behavior; it does not attempt value judgments as to what the goals of education should be. The function of philosophy is to show the way to go; the job of educational psychology is to tell the teacher the best way to get there. The teacher who believes a highly competitive society impractical will use only forms of competition that do not interfere with interpersonal relationships.

We have seen that competition is an effective form of motivation with children, but that its usefulness is limited by its disruptive effect on individual morale and on group interaction. The task becomes one of finding out what form of social motivation can be used within the limits of the ultimate social good, and of determining the conditions under which it is most effective.

The teacher often has to decide whether to have children work individually or in pairs or in larger groups. If she uses groups, shall she select them herself, or let the class choose, or let individuals volunteer? How large should a group be for the best work? Will the individual be submerged in the group and fail to learn? What are the guide lines by which to set up the most effective groups? All of these are practical questions.

Two major areas of research are available. The first has to do with the relative effectiveness of competition and cooperation, what the conditions are under which individuals will learn from the group, and what kinds of groups result in the best kind of motivation for children. The second has to do, not with what the participants learn, but with how good the group judgment or product will be.

In research on cooperation as a form of social motivation, co-

operation is defined as interdependent behavior varying from so-
liciting help from others to carrying on activities with regard for
and dependence upon others. It is similar to competition in that
there is active and continuing contact with other children, but it
differs in that the contact is designed toward mutual reinforcement
rather than toward excelling or dominating.

Such studies seem to show:

1. *Cooperation may or may not be less effective than competition.
Results are inconclusive, depending on the type of task or goal.* The
child is more highly motivated by work for self than he is by work
for the group, although with experience in group work he comes to
respond equally to the two forms of motivation. The balance that
team rivalry provides between cooperation within the group and
competition against another group combines the effectiveness of
work for self with the social gains of work for the group.

2. *The quality of interpersonal relations under cooperation is
positive, that under competition is negative.* Individual reward
under competition is associated with increased variability of behavior, attacks on others, and increased speed of work without corresponding increase in quality. Cooperation, on the other hand,
leads to positive responses toward others, social freedom, group
identification, greater interdependence of behavior, and in general
more socialized forms of behavior. Cooperation seems to have a
more lasting effect than competition.

3. *Groups which work best together are relatively small, homogeneous, self-chosen, and familiar.* Those who have something in
common can understand each other better, whether the common
factor is an interest in building a store or the ability to read.
Learners of the same sex work together better than those of opposite
sex. Groups in which the individual chooses to work with certain
others cooperate more easily than those which the teacher assigns, or
even those in which the chairman chooses the participants. Groups
of individuals who know and like each other accomplish more work
than those that disregard such spontaneous choices.

4. *Cooperation is a more advanced stage of social development
than competition.* It occurs more often among older students than
among younger, though even animals cooperate. It occurs only as
the result of training, however. It is particularly important for
teachers to aid the development of cooperation. Cooperation is re-

lated to imitativeness and the seeking of approval, rather than to direct domination and direction over others.

Here the development of the social personality is illuminating. The infant at first is autistic, thinking only of self and the other-than-self as the other serves his needs. He gradually learns to distinguish people from things, and to find that they have their own directions rather than always being at his service. He then begins to enjoy parallel play, doing the same things others do without inter-action (social facilitation). He later tries to eliminate or use or dominate others in attaining his own ends (competition); and eventually he learns to identify or feel with others and to be content only if they, too, are attaining their objectives (cooperation). Only when he learns to identify with others is he fully mature socially.

. . . IN THE CLASSROOM

These facts suggest that the teacher should use small interacting groups in the classroom whenever they are appropriate to the activity undertaken. Committee work is good for promoting social stimulation and needed learnings. The groups which are formed should be relatively small, only large enough to represent all the skills needed to do the job.

Going back to the unit on pioneer life described earlier, let us see how the teacher set up the working groups:

After we had the list of things we wanted to do on the board, we started setting up the working groups. For each one we discussed first what the group would be expected to do, and what skills the people working on the group would need. Then I asked for volunteers. We did this for each task in turn. Sometimes the class decided it was something everyone should do; sometimes they felt that not more than two or three people could work well on such a job; but we listed all the people who wanted to work anyway.

That night I did some checking to see what children had been left out, and added each name to the group where the child could work best. I also did some checking to see which names were duplicated, crossing them off where they were least needed.

The next day I took my list back to the class for discussion. They suggested a few shifts of assignment. I then asked the child whom I thought of as strongest in each group to see that they got started to work, and they broke up into their groups to plan. I moved about helping as I could. At the end of the hour each group reported what it had decided to do first, and asked for help on any problems that had arisen.

I purposely failed to appoint a chairman. Teachers can be so wrong about who the real leader in a group may be, Instead, I let the leadership emerge as they worked together. Often it was not the child I had asked to get things started, but someone I had completely underestimated.

Throughout the whole procedure, the nature of the work to be done and the skills of the members were emphasized, resulting in a group relatively homogeneous in ability and interest for each task.

A problem that teachers often have to meet is that of deciding whether to let students work with their friends and what to do about cliques. Such groups are common in adolescence. One seventh-grade teacher tells of her experience:

All the girls who came from one of the elementary schools wanted to work together, play together, and have lunch together. In fact, they had agreed to do this for mutual protection before leaving the elementary school. It became something of a problem in classes.

One of my colleagues thought the way to handle it was to explain to the girls that they needed to make new friends, and to always place them on committees where none of their friends were present. I tried that once or twice, but they spent their time looking around for their friends, or trying to talk with them and restlessly moving about.

So I decided on a different way to work. I asked one of them whether another girl, new to the school, might have lunch with them for a few days until she got acquainted with people. They liked her, and made her one of them permanently. On committees, I let two or three of them work together, along with others from other groups, gradually increasing the proportion of others. With the help of the playground and activities programs, they relinquished their clique and spent time with many different girls.

THE CO-WORKING GROUP

There remains the final question concerning how good is the work done by a group compared with that done by an individual, not what the effects are on the individual who cooperates or competes. This question is really at the heart of much of our social philosophy. Does democracy, in the sense of group-made decision, result in a workable, a wise decision? Or would it be better to simply find the best minds and turn all our problems over to them? The question of social philosophy is an important one, and the teacher has the problem of whether the gains from the group situa-

. . . IN THE CLASSROOM

These findings mean that the teacher is on sound footing when she stresses group work, particularly in problem-solving types of activity. In planning a unit of work on a given country, the teacher will encourage children to look at pictures and talk with people and read and observe widely, then bring the class together to pool information and plan the work. On the basis of group decision, work will be allocated to individuals who will indicate their preferences to the group and carry their individual tasks forward. They will report back to the group for criticism and suggestions.

Students usually work in small groups of two or three. Here they have the advantage of social motivation and increased range of ideas, with a minimum of complexity in planning. When such small committees constitute the work groups, they usually report to the class frequently for criticism and suggestion.

Again, using the class as a group is helpful in handling certain kinds of discipline problems. There may be disorder in getting started to work, or in cleaning up, or in entering and leaving the classroom. The teacher's impulse is to try to figure out the best solution and to impose it on the group. A more effective technique is to bring the problem to the class for discussion and for working out a plan of action. The teacher states the problem in an impersonal way so that the self-respect of every individual is safeguarded. The teacher contributes to the discussion as a member of the group, but not as director. Usually the solution found is better than what the teacher alone might have devised, and gains greater support from the class since the members had a hand in making it. The teacher must be content to let the group try its own solution even if it rejects her suggestion; if the group plan does not work, class discussion can be opened again.

In committee work with adult groups the same principles apply. A small committee, perhaps of three to five, is likely to yield more results per member than a very large one, though if the task is very complex there will be an increased range of ideas in the larger committee. As one teacher puts it:

The trick is to get everybody working. Sometimes they are not especially interested, sometimes they do not have much time, sometimes they are uncertain of their own ability. As chairman I used to make the mistake of trying to have everything planned out in advance and just asking for group approval. But that isn't the best way.

Now I just start the meeting by stating what the job is that we have to do. I let them toss the idea around and ask questions, get tired of wasting time and raise the question of how to proceed. Then I am ready with a few suggestions of alternative ways we might go to work. By that time they are ready to talk, to criticize what I have said, and make other suggestions of their own. Eventually we come out with some sort of plan that is different from the plan any one of us took to the meeting in the first place.

Often they take over the planning for themselves at that point, saying "I can do that," or "I'll help, but I think someone else could do that better." Sometimes I have to ask for volunteers and for nominations. But each person takes on some job as his own. The chairman has his hands full just refereeing and anticipating the probable next steps.

Briefly, a cooperating group not only stimulates the individuals in the group but also gets work of better quality done. This fact, added to the necessity for helping children learn cooperation to live in the modern world, makes providing opportunities for cooperative work in the classroom essential.

SOCIAL CLASS AND ETHNIC GROUPS AND LEARNING

All of us are increasingly concerned with the learning problems of students from areas variously called "culturally disadvantaged," "socially deprived," "ghetto," or "mid-city." We have already called attention to level of aspiration as a primary problem there. There are others.

Such students usually come from families where there has been relatively little schooling, direct experiences are limited, vocabularies are limited, reading is a task rather than a habit, and "school" is at best a meaningless institution. The child comes to school with few resources to help in his academic learning, and sometimes with negative attitudes. This complex means that, from "Head Start" before kindergarten to "Upward Bound" in the twelfth grade, the school must provide experiences and must give more than ordinary help toward using language fluently and reading widely, building success into the whole sequence. If the school fails in a middle-class area, parents will grumble but pick up the task of educating their children. If it fails in an impoverished area, the parents and children have no alternative resource.

Yet the learning of children in such communities is much like that of others, covered by the principles suggested here for all children. It is only that the elements of learning differ in stress, both on experiential and motivational factors. Those factors are pointed out in appropriate sections. And good learning opportunities are essential; such schools cannot afford to fail.

IMPLICATIONS

We may, then, conclude that the teacher should:

1. Use the classroom audience to increase the strength of motivation. Avoid over-motivation through use of the audience. Avoid using negative forms of motivation before an audience. Make sure the learner understands and prepares for his audience. Use the audience in lifelike ways. Use the audience chiefly when speed is desired.

2. Use competition chiefly as self-competition against the student's own record. Avoid competition between individuals. Avoid over-motivation through competition. Make the competition easy enough that the learner can succeed. Use competition chiefly where speed or overlearning is important.

3. Use cooperative group work often. Use group work chiefly with other students. Use cooperation for problem solving and where quality of work is important. Form groups that are small and homogeneous; follow social attractions; and give students some chance to choose.

4. Plan carefully for the more capable learner in group situations. Use audience and competitive situations very little. Let him work with students of similar ability often. Respect his desire for individual work and self-direction.

EXERCISES IN APPLICATION

1. Paul is an able, aggressive, cheerful boy in the fifth grade. Jane is a normal but quiet and somewhat solitary girl in the same class. The teacher tells the class that desks must be cleaned up and made more orderly, mentioning Paul and Jane as illustrations of people with messy desks. What is likely to be the reaction of Paul? Of Jane?

2. A teacher asks that a boy, who has some interesting information about the topic being studied, report it to the class. Other students find they also want to tell the class about something they know, until the discussion becomes so active that students are interrupting each other. The teacher says, "Let's all write our stories and go over them together later." What learning principle or principles is the teacher using?

3. An instructor assigned a term paper in history, which you turned in and he graded as A. As he returned it to you he asked you to summarize it for the class and to answer their questions. What is the nature of your feeling about this request? How well will you do? Why?

4. A high-school science teacher is interested in building strong interest in his subject. Will this objective be better achieved by assigning experiments to an individual or to co-working groups? Why?

5. Larry was one of the brightest children in the class, and he liked to work with others. When he was placed in a group to plan a report to the class, what was the effect on the work of the other children in terms of quality? And on the quality of the joint report? Why?

6. In solving a series of difficult problems in arithmetic, what kind of learner is likely to do his best work alone? The slow-learning or the bright student? The beginner or the one with more background?

7. A fifth-grade teacher is setting up a group to work on a mural for exhibition to parents at open house. What process will it be best to use? Teacher assignment or class volunteers? Good artists or a heterogeneous group? A group of three or a group of eight? A group of friends or a group of people who seldom play or work together? Why?

8. Compare the effect of social facilitation when studying in the library and when studying on a playground.

9. What is the effect of competition on quality and quantity of work? Which is the more effective competition, against another individual or against a group? Is granting a handicap wise?

10. What constitutes a group which will work well together? How can a teacher use this fact? Illustrate.

SUGGESTIONS FOR FURTHER READING

Boocock, S. S. "Toward a Sociology of Learning." *Soc. of Educ., 39,* 1–45, 1966. A review of research on the sociology of learning, including classroom structure and techniques, peer groups, and external social groups.

Bowers, N. D. "Meaningful Learning and Retention: Task and Method Variables." *Rev. Educ. Res., 31,* 522–534, 1961. A review of task and method variables in teaching including level of difficulty, ordering, meaning, recitation, and classroom grouping.

Deutsch, Cynthia P. "Education for Disadvantaged Groups." *Rev. Educ. Res., 35,* 140–146, 1965. A review of the literature on the "disadvantaged," stressing the importance of positive concern with educational programs for developing potentialities.

Gagné, R. M. "Problem-Solving and Thinking." *Ann. Rev. Psych., 10,* 147–172, 1959. A somewhat technical review of psychological literature on learning, 1954–1958, including sections on decision making and the co-working group.

Gordon, Edmund W. "Characteristics of Socially Disadvantaged Children." *Rev. Educ. Res., 35,* 377–387, 1965. A review of the research on the socially disadvantaged, emphasizing learning characteristics in such groups.

Grotberg, Edith H. "Learning Disabilities and Remediation in Disadvantaged Children." *Rev. Educ. Res., 35,* 413–425, 1965. Suggestions for the development of a theoretical system within which the research on remediation in such groups may be examined.

Hare, A. P., E. F. Borgatta, and R. F. Bales. *Small Groups: Studies in Social Interaction.* New York: Knopf, 1965. A series of theoretical and research articles on topics such as group influence, size and leadership.

Jensen, A. L. "Social Class and Perceptual Learning." *Mental Hyg., 50,* 226–239, 1966. A survey of research on the effect of social environment on brain capacity and learning ability, with implications for educating the underprivileged.

Lorge, I., and others. "A Survey of Studies Contrasting the Quality of Group Performance and Individual Performance." *Psych. Bull., 55,* 337–372, 1958. A comprehensive survey comparing group and individual performance on several variables.

Mann, R. D. "A Review of the Relationships between Personality and Performance in Small Groups." *Psych. Bull., 56,* 241–270, 1959. A review of personality variables in group work.

The Material to Be Learned

One of the important functions of the teacher is to select the learning experiences and organize the material to be learned. She must often decide whether a given learning unit is too long and too complex, and if so how to simplify it without destroying any of its meaning. She must decide how long to work on a given activity, and how to break the learning periods so that there is the greatest gain from a change of activity. She must organize material, and decide where to start in presenting it and what guidelines to follow. Though these issues about material in the specific sense are the concern of specialists in curriculum, certain general psychological principles apply.

The literature on learning includes a number of pertinent topics. The effects on learning of length, complexity of material, and serial position within the unit, have received careful study. The importances of meaning, familiarity, and context have been explored. So has the whole-part problem, which is of importance since it deals with the internal structure and external relationships of the best unit for learning. Even the studies of extensive and intensive reading have a bearing on the topic.

Let us examine each of these areas in turn and see what it has to contribute to the question of what kind of unit the teacher should select for presenting to her class.

SERIAL POSITION

The teacher often asks a student to perform a series of acts that are just about the same. This kind of task is especially common in learning skills such as spelling or arithmetic. This sameness of isolated and discrete acts sometimes creates special problems in learning. Whenever there is a "series," the teacher is concerned with the relative strength of different positions in the series, that is, with the likelihood that an item in one or another position will be readily learned. In other words, within any relatively independent yet internally monotonous task (for example, learning a list of twenty words) there are strong and weak positions.

Perhaps some of these facts and their interrelationships will be clearer after trying a learning task. Below are several rows of numbers. Get a sheet of blank paper, a pencil, and a small card to help keep the place. Put the card under the first row, concentrate on each number in turn, saying it once aloud and stopping for one second. Cover up the row and write it on the blank piece of paper. Do the same thing for each row, allowing only one second of concentration for each number, and not looking ahead or back.

Now check by circling each number that is right and in the right order. All the numbers in the first series are probably right, perhaps in the second also. When the first errors occurred, in what serial positions were they? Compare the number right in the last series with the number right in the first row.

6, 2, 8, 0, 1, 9
4, 7, 5, 1, 8, 3, 6
5, 4, 8, 6, 3, 0, 7, 2
8, 1, 6, 0, 3, 7, 2, 5, 4
3, 1, 6, 9, 4, 7, 1, 5, 8, 0
6, 1, 3, 7, 2, 5, 1, 0, 4, 6, 9
7, 5, 2, 1, 3, 8, 5, 0, 1, 9, 4, 7

A number of aspects of serial position have been studied. Such studies seem to show that:

1. *The order of learning determines the order of easiest recall.* There is some degree of association between any member and the other members of a series, both adjacent and remote, following and preceding. The strongest linkage, however, is with the adjacent forward position; intermediate linkage occurs with remote forward and with adjacent backward positions; and the weakest linkage is that with the remote backward positions. That is, *l* makes us

think *m* immediately; we may also think *n* or *k;* and if pressed we may also think of *j.* We tend to recall material in the structure in which it was learned. This tendency means that serial order in learning must be varied if we wish mastery of the independent units regardless of context.

2. *The first and last positions in a series are the strongest.* As one student put it, our minds "sag in the middle"; that is, there is a bow-shaped relation between serial position and the effectiveness of learning. This relation holds not only for memory of the units concerned but also for the tension engendered by effort to learn. There has been much discussion as to whether the first or last position is the stronger. The first extends over a number of units while the last is more sharply defined. The first has the advantage when recall must be in the order of learning, the last when free recall in any order is permitted. In general, strength of first and last positions indicates that the end positions are both favorable for learning.

3. *The middle positions in a series are weak.* The studies of learning curves for individual items in different serial positions show that curves for the end positions climb rapidly and those for the middle positions first climb, then level off. This difference might be expected from the relative difficulty of learning in those positions. Differences between serial positions decrease in time, however.

4. *The extent to which differences occur varies with many factors.* Instruction to give special attention to the middle positions strengthens those positions. If free recall is allowed, finality will be stressed; if it is not, primacy dominates. The difference between end and middle positions decreases under distributed practice and increases under massed practice. Rapid presentation brings greater disparity in serial positions than slow presentation. Individuals who have had much practice in learning show less variation with serial position than beginners. Very long lists produce greater dropping in the middle positions than short ones. Monotonous material shows greater discrepancy between serial positions than varied material.

The character of these findings is illustrated in Figure 3, which shows the sharp drop in the middle positions on the first trial, gradually rising with more practice to nearly equal mastery at the level indicated by the fifth trial. Differences level out because of

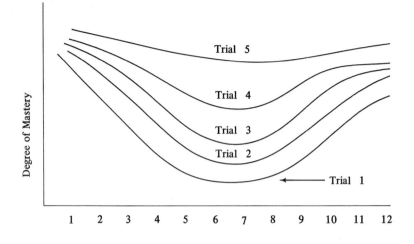

more practice on the middle positions and the normal blending of experiences into a whole.

. . . IN THE CLASSROOM

Simple as these facts are, they have much meaning in teaching. The teacher will vary the order of presentation wherever a specific skill is to be isolated from others. A word must occur in many different contexts before the learner will recognize it independently. If the student learns to spell a list of words in a given order, he should be tested on them in a different order since he must be able to spell regardless of context.

The child will learn his arithmetic combinations first by using reference tables for number facts in solving problems, thus finding the same combinations in many different contexts. If he learns instead to recite them in sequence he may have to go through the whole table to find the one he needs.

He learns his alphabet by using it as a file for spelling words or by looking up words in a dictionary or by filing cards for the classroom library. He will then be able to use the alphabet forward or backward, and to quickly find positions either near or remote from his point of entry. He will not have to repeat the whole alphabet to find the right location. He will learn the number of days in the different months directly by always dating his papers, and not have to rely on such devices as counting knuckles or reciting "Thirty days hath . . ."

The teacher will also break any series in as many ways as she can. Within the period, activities will be varied frequently. She will give an individual meaning to each arithmetic fact and to each word in spelling or reading. She will present a fact or process briefly, move away to something else, and come back to it again and again until it is mastered instead of staying with it too long at one time.

She will use the initial and final positions for points she wishes to stress. Where assignments are given, the beginning and end of the lesson are good positions. In less formal situations, the beginning of the activity may be used for preview and the end for review, with the middle positions for elaboration. One successful lecturer said the secret of his success in a fifty-minute lecture lay in spending ten minutes telling his audience what he was going to tell them, thirty minutes telling them, and ten minutes telling them what he had told them. Such a formula has implications for teachers in other than "telling" situations.

These facts also mean that the teacher must be conscious of her own tendency to present material in the form in which she learned it. Having greatly enjoyed her course in American History, she may try to teach it to her fifth grade just as it was presented to her. She may try to duplicate a unit of work that went over so well with the last class. Instead, she must rearrange and reorganize the material to fit the interests and objectives and abilities of each new class. Material can never be taught in just the same way we learned it, but must always be reorganized and adapted.

LENGTH AND COMPLEXITY

We have said that a very long series has more middle positions and hence more positions difficult for learning. In the number series in the preceding section, those that had too many digits were learned with fewer right than those with just the right quantity.

The effects of length and complexity of material on learning have received attention in psychological research. Such studies lead us to the conclusion that:

1. *Each person has a relatively fixed normal memory span.* By memory span we mean the number of items he can reproduce immediately after a single exposure. How large his memory span will be depends on character of the material, rhythm of presentation, rate of presentation, method of scoring the responses, fatigue, degree of attention, distribution of practice, spontaneous grouping of units, prior familiarity with the material, and his own age, sex, intelligence, and cultural background.

2. *As the amount of like material increases beyond a learner's memory span, the difficulty of learning it increases disproportionately.* The relationship between complexity and learning difficulty is not a directly proportional one, but nearer to the square or the cube of the complexity. The increase is more evident in accuracy scores than in time required. The increased difficulty is present for both verbal and motor learning. Forgetting is also much more rapid for long units. The reason for the rapid rise in difficulty may lie in the fact that each member of a series is related in some degree to every other member, so that adding one unit adds many interfering associations.

3. *As the complexity of material of a given length is increased, the difficulty of learning it increases disproportionately faster.* What we said about length applies also to complexity. With increasing complexity the method of attack on the part of the learner shifts from logical to illogical. The effect of increased complexity is greater for material that must be learned verbatim than for logical and ideational tasks. Forgetting is also disproportionately more rapid for complex forms. When an attempt is made to pack more information into a given time, learning is not significantly increased and it may be disrupted.

4. *Long and complex series can be best learned by grouping, organizing, and forming concepts.* There is a tendency for the individual to organize material into patterns. If no pattern is present in the material itself, the learner's best procedure is to invent one for himself. This can be done through relating ideas and organizing in relation to them, or by grouping. The mnemonic device of forming a word of the first letters of the subtopics as an aid in

memorizing points for a speech illustrates the advantage of grouping.

. . . IN THE CLASSROOM

These facts mean that school tasks that are too complex for the learner not only fail to teach him the extra facts presented but also interfere with those he could easily learn. Learning tasks should be easily within his ability to grasp. They should be simple in design and well structured. He should have plenty of time for assimilation and for forming his own concepts; too often we adults make learning difficult for children by hurrying them.

Illustrations of the meaning of such concepts are found in many simple classroom situations. A child can learn to write a word correctly much more easily by having the teacher help him underline syllables as he says them than by trying to remember the individual letters, because he has fewer units to remember. Try for yourself to remember the spelling of a word we will call "tsnukebierhcszruK," meaning "shorthand." It is, like remembering the many-digit series you learned earlier, relatively difficult. Then turn the same letters around, and pronounce "Kurzschreibekunst" syllable by syllable, looking at each one as you say it. You will find writing the second form easier, since the letter groupings are familiar and you have only four groups to remember.

A young college instructor illustrates the hazard of presenting too much. He says:

> Teaching statistics has always fascinated me, and especially calculating the mean from a frequency distribution. It is logical, and showing that logic is a delight.
>
> Today I tried it. The class already knew how to get an average (or mean) from a series of numbers, and how to group numbers into a frequency distribution. I showed them how to guess about where the mean would fall in a distribution, compute deviations, multiply by the frequencies, correct the estimate and multiply by the size of the interval. They followed fairly well, though a little slowly.
>
> But I had just warmed up. To show the logic I chose another interval, and repeated the process, coming out with the same answer but having larger numbers with which to work. They were puzzled.
>
> Then I suggested that we work from the bottom interval, just as a check on the other two processes. To me it seemed the climax in the development of a logical argument. But there was open, though courteous, revolt. "Please," said one student, "won't you stop? Don't give us any more. Just

let us work some for awhile. I can get it this far, but if you give me any more I'm lost."

Similarly, the teacher may be tempted to teach not only the major outline of the process of long division but also its many variations, all in one day; or to teach both a process and its proof; or to give all the detailed directions for a given activity at once. She may have a young child continue reading until he has more new words than he can assimilate. As a result she will confuse him, and he will lose what learning might have occurred with simpler and shorter presentation. It is important to preserve the outline of the major organization of the learning, as in teaching long division, but many of the details can be omitted at first.

DEGREE OF MEANINGFUL ORGANIZATION

We have seen that as the length and complexity of the material increase beyond the level at which the individual can work easily, the difficulty of learning increases disproportionately. We have also seen, however, that it is possible to increase the level of complexity at which we can work by trying to organize seemingly disparate bits of material around some kind of central concept. In learning the number code in Chapter 4, it would have been easier to learn it as a very simple design, thus:

Instead, there were nine different line combinations, thus:

The mere fact that, by organizing the symbols in a certain way, there was one idea instead of nine to master makes it easier to remember this code.

The importance of meaning can be illustrated still more graphically by learning two verses. Get blank sheets of paper and pencils ready. Read "The Little Turtle" once, aloud and slowly. Close the book and try to write it. Turn back and check. Repeat this process until the verse is complete without error. Then read the "Nonsense Verse" once aloud slowly, close the book, and try to write it. Turn back and check. Repeat this process until the verse is complete without error.

The Little Turtle[1]

There was a little turtle.
He lived in a box.
He swam in a puddle.
He climbed on the rocks.

Nonsense Verse[2]

Inka rima rinka ro,
Banim bokie salib so,
Bick bock, sec sim,
Thigger thogger donner dim.

The two verses are comparable in length and complexity. There are 20 words in the meaningful verse and 16 in the nonsense poem, 17 different words in the meaningful verse and 16 in the nonsense poem, and 23 syllables in the meaningful verse and 25 in the nonsense poem. Compare the number of times it was necessary for you to read each verse in order to remember it. The meaningful verse probably took one or two readings. The nonsense verse probably took many more than that, perhaps six or seven. At that, this particular nonsense verse approaches meaning, since it has rhyme and rhythm, and uses conventional English syllables. If the task had been nonsense prose or Sanskrit poetry, the learning time would have been increased. In other words, the presence of meaning makes a great deal of difference in how easily material can be mastered.

Research in this area includes both laboratory and classroom studies. From such data we may infer that:

1. *Meaningful material is learned more quickly and retained longer than nonsense material.* Even nonsense syllables which are conceptualized are mastered more readily than those which are learned simply as nonsense syllables. In the learning of a foreign

[1] Reprinted with permission of The Macmillan Company from *Collected Poems* by Vachel Lindsay. Copyright 1920 by The Macmillan Company. Renewed in 1948 by Elizabeth C. Lindsay.

[2] Ballard, P. B. "Oblivescence and Reminiscence." *British Journal of Psychology Monograph Supplements, 1, 7,* 1913.

vocabulary, mastery is more rapid if the English equivalents have meaning for the learner than if they do not. The degree of meaning which is present in any material ranges from purely nonsense material, to words, to words in meaningful sequence, to narrative or rhythmic poems. It is four to twenty times easier to learn words in meaningful sequence than to learn them as discontinuous material. Forgetting of nonsense material is much more rapid than forgetting of meaningful material; sometimes, meaningful material shows no loss or even a slight gain over long periods of time.

2. *Similarly, logical learning (learning of essential ideas) is faster and more permanent than verbatim learning.* Forming logical concepts and understanding principles aid both learning and retention, whether the material is meaningful or meaningless, common or uncommon. Logical learning consists of organizing or reorganizing material. If the learner can fit a new item into an existing overall concept, it is no longer confusing. Logical learning transfers to later rote learning more than rote learning does to logical; therefore memorizing should come *after* understanding, not before. The superiority of logical learning varies with the degree of integration of the learning material, being greatest with complex material.

Verbatim learning, on the other hand, requires more trials for learning, more time, and more time per unit. Difficulty increases very rapidly with increasing amount or complexity of material. Verbatim learning shows little transfer to other learning. It is dominated by such mechanical factors as contiguity rather than by ideas. Drill and overlearning are important in rote learning, unimportant in logical learning.

3. *Differences between logical and rote learning, sense and nonsense material, are differences of degree rather than kind.* Some investigators have suggested that different factors operate for substance learning and verbatim learning, but it is probable that the latter simply places different relative weight on the various factors affecting learning. Because logical learning and sense material on the one hand, and rote learning and nonsense material on the other, stand at the extremes of a continuum, it is not safe to generalize directly from one to the other even though there is a relationship.

4. *New learnings should be presented in a familiar context.* Sense and logic in learning come via transfer from past experience. Material is seldom inherently meaningful or logical in itself, but is so because it is partially learned. Learning in context is more rapid

than learning in isolation, particularly when the context is familiar. Material which is learned in a commonplace context is learned more readily than that learned in an unusual context.

5. *Material to be learned should be structured in some orderly or logical fashion.* Learning is not a passive chaining together of adjacent items but rather an active, analytic mode of responding. When meaning is not easily available the individual may speed learning by searching for meaning, by imposing rhythm and pattern, by grouping items, by noting spatial relations, or by reviewing his experiences. Assimilating the new into existing patterns of response will aid learning. Students prefer well-organized subject matter presented with clear objectives; they dislike learning unrelated facts. Closely related material is learned more easily than loosely related material. Highly unitary form facilitates learning, and the failure of form to emerge retards learning.

Grouping increases the span of apprehension so that units can be inferred from the pattern. Individuals seem to spontaneously attempt organization of material; they set up clear and well-structured and interrelated systems in order to learn. Once set up, such configurations resist change; having once learned an organization for material, an individual finds it more difficult to learn a new organization than to learn entirely new material. Allowing the individual to select his own plan of structuring material is superior to imposing structure upon him. He must, however, somehow systematize what is presented, or the material will be ignored, forgotten, isolated, or transformed to fit his preconceived pattern of thought. The advantage of presenting material with organization and structure is even greater in delayed recall than in immediate learning, especially when recall is asked in an organized form.

6. *Individual differences in ability to use rote and logical learning are marked.* Meaningful material and logical learning are especially advantageous for persons high in ability (potential) and low in achievement (actual performance). Drill or rote learning has a greater advantage for those low in ability and relatively high in achievement. There are also differences related to intelligence, age, sex, scholarship, rapidity of presentation of the learning material, type of material, serial position, sensory mode of presentation, feeling tone, guidance, number of repetitions, spacing of practice, reminiscence, and retroactive inhibition.

The difference between learning meaningless and logically related material is illustrated in Figure 4. Quite apart from the ease

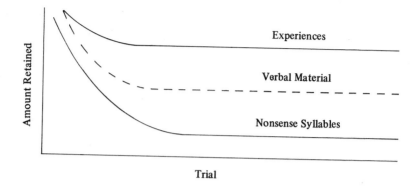

FIGURE 4. MEANING LEADS TO IMPROVED RETENTION

of learning, material that has more structure and form (verbal material) and that which invites the learner to form his own concepts (experiences) show greater permanence of learning than that which is meaningless.

. . . IN THE CLASSROOM

These facts have many implications for teaching. They mean that the best unit for learning is not always the shortest but is rather the most compact, structured, or meaningful. When starting a new learning, we should help the learner to recall related meanings he may have partly forgotten. We should help him to form a structure at the beginning about which to build his learnings. We should stress generalizations and meanings, and use drill only after he clearly understands meanings.

In the primary grades, the child approaches reading through talking about something he has seen or something he wants to do. Sentences are lifted from his conversation and placed on charts as initial reading material. After he understands the context and the meanings of individual phrases, he is asked to relate the visual symbols (or printed words) to what he is saying, that is, to "read" the material. He learns more easily in this way than if he were asked to learn letters or syllables, which have no clear meanings behind them.

When arithmetic processes are taught, the learner is helped first to understand the specific situations from which the problem arose, next to analyze it for a method of solving it. Only then is he taught the symbols by which that process is represented on paper, and still later given drill. He may use the multiplication table as a reference for some time in solving problems before he is asked for recall of all the multiplication facts. To ask him to memorize basic arithmetic facts too early is to give him meaningless material, making his learning of arithmetic much more difficult than it might be if it came from practical problems and from contextual use. In addition, stressing meaning prepares him for later transfer of the material to new situations.

An illustration of stressing meaning in the introduction of an arithmetic process was given by a student observer.

In the arithmetic group, which was working out its problems orally, the teacher dictated problems which all revolved around a little girl's going into a toy store and buying toys. For example, Mary, the little girl, bought a car for twenty-one cents and fish for twenty cents. The children were asked how much money she spent. After determining the sum, they were told that Mary had fifty-five cents when she went into the toy shop, and they were asked how much money she had left.

The subtraction problem was the first that the group had ever attempted. It was presented in a context which was familiar to the children. It had meaning for them, as most of them had been in a toy shop, where they had to determine whether they had enough money for one or more toys. They also had had the experience of receiving change just as Mary did.

To aid in understanding an arithmetic process, another teacher used a context which had meaning and familiarity for the children.

The slow group, who were working on multiplication, seemed to be having trouble. The problem that they were doing was nine times two. The teacher began explaining the concept by addition. They seemed to grasp this idea, so he proceeded by having one of the boys in the group put eighteen paper fish on the flannel board. The fish were in two groups. He then asked one of the girls to write the multiplication problem on the board. She wrote nine times nine and the teacher, knowing that the problem was wrong, asked her how many groups of fishes were on the flannel board. Her answer was two. This made her realize that the multiplication problem was nine times two instead of nine times nine, so she changed the bottom number. The teacher then asked a boy to write the answer. The boy seemed to see the connection between nine plus nine equaled eighteen fishes in two groups and, nine times two, because he quickly wrote eighteen as the answer.

In the teaching of spelling and language rules, the learner begins by writing what he wants to say. As he needs new words or new language forms, the teacher introduces them in context, giving them meaning. Later he practices writing words as spelling. Perhaps he notices that certain words are always used in certain ways and generalizes to language rules. If the statement of rules or the practice in spelling precedes the use of the material in context, learning is much more difficult.

The same concepts reach into the teaching of the social studies and appreciations. Facts about dates, places, events, and persons will be remembered much more easily if each one is given individual meaning. Memorizing such material is difficult and it is quickly forgotten. Memorizing poems or verses for the sake of later appreciation is inefficient; the appreciation should precede the memorization.

If material which is essentially rote in nature must be learned, certain principles for its mastery are useful. For example, spelling is often illogical and inconsistent. To master spelling, many repetitions are needed, preferably in different contexts; thus, the learner must write a great deal. Distribution of practice is important; to learn a word is not enough, but the child must review it periodically, preferably in the normal process of writing new material. When words have been learned recall should be asked in a different order from that in which they were learned; in a spelling list the words should be mixed in order; in composition, the context should be new. The material should be fairly short; the child should have only a few new words to learn each day. Each time, the stress should be on the structure of the word, the constant unit. Words should always be written as wholes, since the word constitutes the unchanging unit in writing rather than the sound or the letter or the phrase. In other words, where meaning is absent, mechanics of presentation and handling are particularly important for the teacher.

WHOLE AND PART LEARNING

All of the preceding facts are closely related to another area of investigation, that of whole and part learning as it applies to the nature of the unit chosen for learning. Though certain aspects of the problem have to do with the timing of learning, let us analyze the whole-part problem in order to see its fundamental relationship to the matter of the meaningfulness and structure of the learning unit.

The teacher must often reach a decision regarding how much of a given body of material she will present at a single time. In memorizing poetry, shall she present the whole poem, or a single stanza, or just a line? In teaching music, shall she sing the whole song each time, or just a phrase, or several phrases? In teaching penmanship, is the best unit the word or the letter or the stroke or the sentence? In teaching piano, shall she teach both hands together from the beginning or each hand separately? All of these are practical questions which have been loosely lumped together as the whole-part problem.

First, let us eliminate from consideration at this time the effects of distribution of practice, though they are interwoven with those of whole and part presentation. It is possible, by coming back to a given learning again and again after rest periods, to teach very difficult and highly complex behaviors; when practice is thus distributed, learning is more efficient than when there is too much drill at a single sitting. But here let us consider only what happens during the first presentation of new material.

In this sense, the problem is what kind of unit the learner can master most easily, and how he should approach that unit for learning. Many investigations have defined *unit* as simply a quantity of material or an additional quantity of the same kind of material, making the problem one of length and complexity. In the preceding section, however, we found that the essence of logical learning is to give structure to that which is relatively unformed. In whole learning we carry that thought one step further.

Here we define a "whole" as a unit which is an organic structure, not an aggregate of small but unrelated parts. It has three primary qualities. (1) It is definitely segregated, relatively independent, isolated, and autonomous, possessing its own characteristic individual entity. (2) It possesses "form-quality," or unity built around a central function. It is an organized, functional unit with decisive internal dynamic relations. It possesses clearness, definiteness, solidarity, regularity, harmony, coherence, and symmetry. (3) It is more than a sum of its parts; it is a rational structure. It is causally coherent, a unit in which changing one section changes the entire structure.

Perhaps the nature of a "whole" in this sense will be clear from the following comparison. We have exactly the same strokes in the two figures illlustrated. In the first they are jumbled, or piled together without form. In the second they have form-quality, or constitute a whole.

Other investigators have applied the whole-part concept to forms of classroom learning. Let us see whether we can generalize from the many studies. They are far from agreement in certain areas, but the following concepts seem to represent the consensus:

1. *Some form of part method is usually preferred by the learner.* The smaller unit requires less initial effort for learning. In addition, the learner experiences a feeling of success each time he masters a part, and the total of the success experiences for many parts is greater than the single feeling of success he achieves in working from the beginning with the whole material. Part learning shows rapid initial learning of the parts themselves, but does not transfer to the whole.

2. *Units should be clearly and simply structured or patterned.* Learning is not a process of reproducing what is presented, but one of invention and reconstruction—of understanding whole-qualities through improved organization of the material. Difficulty in learning is a function of the amount of re-forming or structuring that the material requires to become meaningful to the learner. The concept of what constitutes a whole is a relative rather than an absolute one. A whole for a given child depends upon his purpose in learning, his maturity, the meaningfulness of the material to him, the closeness of logical relationships or continuity within the unit, and the situation in which the learning will ultimately be used. Whole presentation is superior especially for bright children. It has an advantage in creating interest, in transferring to new situations,

and in long-term retention. It favors understanding and carries the benefits that accompany understanding.

3. *Where the unit is structured but overcomplex for the learner, it is best to present the major outline, then isolate one part for attention, then fit it back into the unit within the same learning situation.* If the learning must ultimately be used in the context of the whole, too complete learning of parts may inhibit later learning of the whole; part learning does not transfer automatically to the whole. It is well to begin by doing the thing in the way in which it is eventually to be done, but in major outline uncomplicated by too many details; then to isolate each part for special attention; then to link the parts back to the whole structure.

The learner himself should help in structuring and organizing the materials, selecting problems and evolving plans, solution and evaluation. If he gains the idea of the pattern of the whole, he will fill in the appropriate parts. For example, a student in writing a story needs a word he cannot spell; the teacher shows him how to write it; he uses it and goes on with the story. Later he places that word on his spelling list and studies it: isolation of the part is helpful in mastery. Still later he needs the word again in writing stories, and either recalls or looks it up and writes it again until he recalls it.

4. *Conversely, where there is no inherent connection between learnings, they should be taught as independent units.* It is most effective to teach together those things that belong together, to teach separately those things that do not belong together. Teachers sometimes think that everything they do should be fitted into a major unit of work, but find that such things as holidays or some aspects of arithmetic do not fit in. Independent minor units should be devised for such needed learnings, but without forcing the relationship. Wherever the material to be learned resists organization, is of unequal difficulty or irregular in nature, must remain relatively meaningless or "blind," or where it is very long, part learning is about as effective as whole learning. Where two or more small units exist, with stronger internal relations than the ties between them, teaching them separately (that is, following the structure of each unit) will be superior. There is no merit in grouping unrelated units together.

5. *Individual differences and differences in procedure affect the results of learning activities.* Older students can understand more complex wholes. Brighter pupils learn especially well by being

exposed to wholes, because they are mentally more mature and tend to approach learning more logically. Learners who have had experience with whole learning can use that approach more effectively than those who are accustomed to learning by parts. Children who are emotionally disturbed have difficulty with whole learning, just as they have difficulty with long or complex material, because their general learning impairment makes it difficult to grasp large relationships. The relative superiority of whole learning also varies with the type, difficulty, nature, and length of the material; with the amount, distribution, and nature of practice; with the form of the part method used; and with the method of measuring and the length of interval between learning and checking retention.

In summary, we can assume there is a general level of complexity of material which is best for a given learner. What that level is will depend on his age, degree of brightness, and purpose in learning. The unit we choose to present to him should have a high degree of rational structure or form-quality from his point of view. Having selected such a unit, we should approach it as a totality at first, then break it down into units as far as may be necessary for mastery at the level required, then return it to the total context.

. . . IN THE CLASSROOM

Illustrations of whole and part learning are numerous in the teaching experience. In preparation for their contribution to the class Christmas program, a group elected to dramatize a story. Instead of dividing the story into sections and learning the parts for which they would be responsible, the students read the whole story through several times, first to refresh their memories concerning the plot as a whole, then to select the parts they wanted to play. Then, to learn their own parts, they reread the whole story as many times as they felt necessary. No attempt was made to learn specific lines; the effort was rather to develop an understanding of the sequence of the action. Each time the group rehearsed the play the dialogue was different. As a result a natural reading situation was used, memorization and tedious rehearsals were avoided, pupils used ingenuity to keep the play moving logically, interest of the players was maintained at a peak, and the class was interested because the group version did not parrot the original.

In teaching the language arts there are many illustrations of whole and part learning. Spelling and penmanship and written language are all parts of the same unit in the primary grades, and writing stories results in improvement in all three. When the child is ready for spelling, penmanship may continue to be a part of the lesson for it also is concerned with exact reproduction of word form. Since the word is the smallest meaningful unit in writing and in spelling, breaking words into syllables for spelling or into letter elements for penmanship has little value; the smaller fragments are meaningless and unstructured, hence difficult to learn and of little transfer value. In teaching sentence structure and language usage, the greatest gain comes from pointing out specific things that are right and wrong in the process of writing rather than through teaching rules that the learner cannot understand and has difficulty in applying. If rules are taught, they should be those the student himself discovers through his experience.

In learning to read or speak a language, the same principles hold. Children are introduced to reading through stories they have themselves written. They read the entire story, then sentences, then phrases. To break down the material beyond the phrase is to destroy the meaning. Studies show that the mental age required for learning to read by alphabetic or phonic methods is greater than that required for a story-unit method. In learning shorthand, beginning with sentences has been shown to be superior to beginning with words or with phonetic elements. In learning typing, beginning with continuous composition is superior to beginning with formal exercises. In learning foreign languages, taking up material in context in the form of reading or speaking is superior to memorizing a vocabulary and declensions and conjugations from the beginning. For example, read the following selection and try to infer the meaning from similar English words, filling in difficult words from context:

Engang det var en mann. Det navn av mann var Jakob. Det mann Jakob sagt, "Jeg vil ha en ny hus. Jeg vil ha en bra, ny hus."

Now check for mastery of the vocabulary below. Probably you had all except one or two words right, simply by inference from context.

av	= of	ha	= have	navn	= name
bra	= good	hus	= house	ny	= new
det	= the, there	Jakob	= Jack	sagt	= said
en	= a	Jeg	= I	var	= was
engang	= once	mann	= man	vil	= will

It is the supporting value of context that gives whole presentation its superiority as the initial step in language teaching.

In teaching languages and spelling, however, momentary isolation for attention has value if the individual word is to be fixed for recall. Studying the vocabulary itself, then again reading the context will fix such relatively foreign words as *bra* and *engang* in the above selection. Studying the spelling of a word, undisturbed by context, will aid its recall the next time it is needed. The word should be met first in context, however, in order to achieve the best results. Elementary teachers, for example, let children meet new words in context in reading, then look them up for meaning or work on them for word recognition, then again find the words in context. In teaching social studies, and natural sciences, and mathematics the same principles apply. The context principle has been widely demonstrated for the teaching of mathematics. Weaving together material about geography and history in a normal interacting context is superior to teaching each separately. Giving longer units of reading and study in history, initiated by a preview to understand the structure of the block of material, is superior to giving daily study-recitation assignments. Teaching history by beginning with the present (the context in which the learner will use the material) has an advantage in initial learning over beginning with the remote past.

In promoting motor skills, essentially the same thing is true. Supervised play is superior to formal gymnastics in promoting general development. In learning to juggle, practice should be on the total process, gradually increasing in complexity, rather than on specific skills.

In music, the importance of whole learning is especially great because of the interdependence of the parts. Students learn piano most effectively by using both hands together from the beginning rather than by learning them separately and combining them. Similarly, they learn piano selections better by repeating the whole section over and over than by repeating phrases, better even than by practicing difficult phrases. As the individual becomes an accomplished musician, however, he can work with parts without losing the concept of the whole; thus with increased mastery the difference between the two ways of learning disappears. Even with mastery, however, the individual learns best when given opportunity for mental prestudy of the selection to understand its structure. A tone occurring alone is judged in a different way from a tone occurring in combination; contrasts seem to be emphasized in combination. In part singing, the teacher first teaches the melody line, preferably with a soft accompaniment indicating the harmony. Then parts are fitted into the total structure. If practice on specific parts is needed, it is done to the accompaniment of piano or soft humming of the melody or the full harmony in approximately the right rhythm to maintain the form of the whole.

The concept of learning as the restructuring of experience is related to a basic premise of the modern school, that learning is essentially problem solving, an active process primarily directed toward understandings, not toward rote memory. In this context "whole" learning takes on new meaning.

EXTENSIVE AND INTENSIVE READING

A related area of research is concerned with whether one or many sources should be used in teaching. It is related to context in the broad and long-term sense. Is it enough to use the text? How many copies of how many different books does a teacher need?

The studies include those of reading in general, of extensive and intensive reading, of order in teaching history, science, literature, and of beginning reading in preprimers. With remarkable unanimity such studies show:

1. *Presenting the same facts in varied contexts results in superior learning.* Extensive reading results in increased interest, voluntary reading, and understanding, and hence in increased retention. It also transfers to solving new problems to a greater degree, and results in mastery of peripheral facts as well as those toward which the learning is directed. Extensive reading should be used in most content fields.

2. *Intensive study results in superior learning only for exact reproduction of the facts stated.* It shows immediate superiority for specific facts, but less retention. Intensive reading has value in such skills as reading directions. It should be taught as a special reading skill.

. . . IN THE CLASSROOM

The use of multitext reading in content fields is, then, a useful practice. In a social-studies lesson, for example, an observer reported:

The class had previously listed on the board the questions for which answers were to be found. The teacher had three or four books on each student's desk when he came in from recess. Each book had a slip in it marking the place where some of the material might be found.

They began reading and noting the answers to questions. After a time, they discussed each question and each gave his answer by reading from his own book. The range in difficulty of reading material was quite apparent, but each had something that he could read easily, as well as the pleasure of bringing something different to class.

More mature students can find their own material through the index, perhaps even find their own books from a classroom library shelf.

Similarly, in learning reading or literature the student should be encouraged to read widely rather than to master a few classics only. In the primary grades, he should meet the same words over and over again in a variety of charts and preprimers instead of reading the same charts or primers repeatedly.

When mastery for exact reproduction is desired, however, using a single source has its advantage. Words are spelled much the same, no matter which text the learner consults; multiple sources provide little or no variety. It is better to stay with one way of doing an arithmetic process until it is mastered. Learning to read a recipe and follow it exactly, a useful skill in life, requires adherence to one recipe at a time. When the class is making adobe brick for building a Mexican house, the teacher may mimeograph instructions and use them as a basis for a lesson in intensive reading.

IMPLICATIONS

1. Vary the order and context in which material is presented. Ask for recall in a different order or context. Use many different sources presenting the same facts. Use intensive study only for memorization or exact reproduction.

2. Use first and last positions in a lesson for overview and emphasis. Use middle positions for elaboration. Vary activities so that there are few "middle" positions.

3. Use material at the learner's normal learning level. Determine each individual's learning potential. Avoid giving him tasks that are too long or too complex *for him*.

4. Choose material that is meaningful for the learner. Present new learnings in a familiar context. Build meanings through ex-

perience and discussion. Encourage the student to look for logical relationships and principles in all types of material. Spend relatively large amounts of time developing concepts, relatively little on drill.

5. Choose learning units that are simply and clearly structured, and follow that structure in presentation. Start by presenting the whole outline. Isolate any segments that must be mastered. Teach separately units that do not "belong" together.

EXERCISES IN APPLICATION

1. Charles is preparing for a television quiz program in which he expects to be asked to name the Presidents of the United States in order. Dagmar, on the other hand, will appear on a competing channel on which she expects to be asked to name in one minute as many Presidents of the United States as she can. What method of preparation would you recommend? Should it differ or be the same? Why?

2. Miss Haven and Mrs. Irish were discussing the best way to present American history in the eighth grade. Miss Haven insisted it was important to include current events, field trips, model elections, and such activities to give meaning to the course. Mrs. Irish felt that following the text with plenty of review would result in better coverage of important points. What learning principle were they really discussing? Whose point of view would you accept?

3. A student has demonstrated that he can learn a French vocabulary of twenty new words in one evening and retain about sixteen of those words for daily use. If the length of the vocabulary learned is increased to forty words, about how many would you expect him to retain? Why? What learning principle operates?

4. Forming the word "WAJM" from the initial letters of the names of the first four Presidents of the United States illustrates facilitating remembering through the use of what learning principle?

5. If a second-grade teacher asked a child to go to the office for a pair of scissors, paste, a red pencil, some rulers, and blue paper, which would he be most likely to forget? Why? What principle is functioning?

6. Miss Krause posted a well-written alphabet above her blackboard as a model, but did not call attention to it in her writing lessons. Miss Lemmon did not even post her alphabet. Will the different plans make any difference in the average handwriting ability of the two classes at the end of the semester, other things being equal? What learning principle does this comparison illustrate?

7. A third-grade teacher is introducing the multiplication facts to her class. Should she use a single text with fairly uniform supplemental mate-

rials, or should she use a multitext approach? Why? Would the same logic apply to her use of reading texts? Why?

8. Mrs. Smith is amazed to find that Bill must go through the whole table of nines to find the result of multiplying nine by nine. What principle does this need illustrate? How could this difficulty have been prevented? How can it be corrected?

9. When a student is first given a poem of three verses to memorize he is likely to try to master the first verse, then the second, then the third, then repeat all. Why? Under what conditions will his choice be a good one, and under what conditions should he go over all three at each reading?

10. A fifth grade learned to name states and their capitals by geographic area. A substitute teacher gave the class a test in which the children were to list the states alphabetically and name the capital of each. How will the scores on this test compare with those on a test given by the regular teacher with geographic organization? Why? What are the implications for teaching factual material?

SUGGESTIONS FOR FURTHER READING

Ausubel, D. B., and D. Fitzgerald. "Meaningful Learning and Retention: Intrapersonal Cognitive Variables." *Rev. Educ. Res., 31,* 500–510, 1961. A three-year summary of research emphasizing variables related to cognitive structure and style, including complexity in relation to teaching at various developmental levels.

Bruner, Jerome S., and others. *Studies in Cognitive Growth.* New York: Wiley, 1966. A collection of studies with children on conceptual strategies, ordering, perception and the like.

Cofer, C. N., and B. S. Musgrove, eds. *Verbal Learning and Verbal Behavior: Problems and Processes.* New York: McGraw-Hill, 1963. A collection of articles on meaningfulness, familiarity, immediate memory, one-trial learning and the like.

Epstein, W., I. Rock, and C. B. Zuckerman. "Meaning and Familiarity in Verbal Learning." *Psych. Monog., 74,* #4, 1960. An analysis of the function of familiarity in learning.

Goulet, L. R. "Verbal Learning in Children: Implications for Developmental Research." *Psych. Bull., 69,* 359–376, 1968. A review of research on verbal learning with reference to developmental research.

Kendler, T. S. "Concept Formation." *Ann. Rev. Psych., 12,* 447–472, 1961. A somewhat technical analysis of the history and content of research on concept formation, touching on complexity, reward, and genetic factors among other topics.

McDonald, F. J. "Meaningful Learning and Retention: Task and Method Variables." *Rev. Educ. Res., 34,* 530–544, 1964. A three-year review of research on variables in learning, touching on learning set, discovery learning, grouping, and related topics.

Meux, M. O. "Studies in Learning in the School Setting." *Rev. Educ. Res.*, *37*, 539–562, 1967. A review of approaches to the study of classroom learning, emphasizing problems of conceptualization and methods.

Underwood, B. J., and R. W. Schulz. *Meaningfulness and Verbal Learning*. Philadelphia: Lippincott, 1960. A summary of research on meaningfulness and its effect on rote learning in children.

The Learning Procedure

Having selected material that is meaningful, well structured, and suited to the learner, the teacher must next decide how to proceed in presenting that material. How can the teacher make the presentation sufficiently vivid that little drill will be needed and that the students will remember a maximum of what is presented each time? How much planning and preparation of materials should the teacher do, and how much should she leave to the class? How much can she assume the children will absorb simply from the presence of objects or routines in the schoolroom environment? She must also make the important decisions on when to help and when not to help, when to give an answer and when to give just enough help to keep the child progressing in his own search for an answer, and what kind of help to give when help is indicated. All of these questions are concerned with how the teacher goes about her task, rather than what kind of learning material she has decided to use.

The discussions of meaning and of whole-part learning in the preceding chapter are pertinent, affecting procedure as well as material. Relatively meaningless material can be made meaningful and therefore easy to learn by associating it with the familiar; and relatively formless material can be given form by searching for structure and logical relationships. We have already observed that the context in which the learning is eventually to be used must be the context in which the specific learning is introduced, and that the specific must later be isolated for attention. Going on from that point, the teacher will find certain other principles of procedure valuable.

VIVIDNESS: SIZE, COLOR, AND MOVEMENT

Many studies of effectiveness in advertising have implications for the teacher in the classroom. The advertiser is interested in influencing human behavior, just as the teacher is. The advertiser, however, can depend only on a small fragment of time, and he must capture the attention of his audience. The teacher has much more time and can demand attention, or at least can rule out many distractors of attention. However, if the teacher employs principles used by the advertiser, the learning process may be speeded.

Think of the advertisements that have attracted your attention; analyze why they were attractive. Some of them were highly colored, perhaps in neon lights. Others were so large they stood out above all others; others, perhaps, very small in the middle of a blank page. Still others were moving, as flashing lights or changing figures or a chalk artist drawing a picture. A series of signs which must be read in turn is akin to movement. Still others led to anticipation of movement by their very nature, as a tall stack of old tires off center at the top looks as if it will fall at any moment on the service station below. A restaurant name seen from the inside is a puzzle to be figured out. Poor grammar or inaccurate spelling in a sign creates a desire to correct the form. All these things claim a high level of attention. Among the experimental studies there have been attempts to determine the effect of absolute and of relative size on the memory for symbols, studies of the presence and placement of color, studies of movement, and the like.

Generalizing from such studies as these, the following principles emerge:

1. *Varying the relative size of a bit of material claims attention.* Relative rather than absolute size is important; the influence is one of novelty and attention value. Using a size that is different from that of the rest of the material introduces pattern and isolation. Relative size attracts attention chiefly in the initial presentation, and quickly loses its effect. Printing everything in large type does not facilitate learning; but printing a given part in *different* size type does aid initial learning of that part.

2. *Presence of a unique color claims attention.* Color is important chiefly as a differentiating factor; if the color is constant throughout the material it has no value. For example, a list of words, all red on

white, has no advantage over a list of words which are all black on white. The extent to which color is effective in attracting attention is a function of the way the color is used rather than of the amount of color; so is the effectiveness of color in creating differentiation and isolation. Red is effective in printing because of its contrast value on a customarily black and white page. Color directs attention to itself rather than to noncolored items, and its effectiveness depends on the relative amount of color on the page. Color is preferred by learners, and the presence of color anywhere on a page raises the attention value of the page as a whole. Some investigators claim that color representation is more realistic than black and white and hence induces a reality set in the learner, as opposed to the autistic or self-oriented set associated with black and white. The use of color attracts attention, makes learning easier, and facilitates retention.

3. *The more the factor of movement is brought into the stimulus pattern, the more effective the learning.* Watching the development of a design introduces eye movement, which facilitates learning. The use of films and television is built on this principle.

4. *Novelty is an important factor in claiming attention.* Unusual size, color, movement, and change produce attention. We have noted the same result for disturbances of timing. Novelty claims attention and hence facilitates the learning of that which is novel.

5. *The more vivid the impression, the less the time needed for drill.* Retention will be better from each vivid presentation than from a less intense form. Vividness may be created through size, color, movement, novelty, sensory appeal, and other devices.

. . . IN THE CLASSROOM

These facts suggest ways in which the teacher can emphasize learnings. In arranging her classroom she can make use of them in catching the student's eye and stimulating his interest. A bowl of bright flowers against a background of the right sort is attractive; but if the class watches the teacher arrange the flowers the children will be still more interested. Pictures with bright colors on the bulletin board, changed regularly, will capture attention. A very small notice mounted on a very large sheet of paper will attract the eye and lead the student to read the notice. A unit on transportation interests him because the materials with which he works move.

In pointing out words of particular importance and in making sure that the emphasis in a given bit of material is wisely placed, the teacher may be able to use such concepts. In each case, whether it be size or color or movement or simply novelty, the important thing to do is to differentiate the particular part for the learner, and to make the impression as intense as possible.

The teacher needs to know, too, how to use wisely the great variety of slides, film strips, kinescopes, tapes, films, and other audiovisual teaching media available. Such media have greater vividness than reading and talking alone, and they are often carefully structured. It is essential to know the resources of the school in relation to the content taught, and to understand how they can be used to introduce a topic or illuminate a point. The teacher will want to see the film or hear the tape before attempting to use it, just as she must know the specific learnings that a programmed workbook covers.

Television, like other audiovisual media, is used increasingly in teaching. Science demonstrations, foreign-language lessons, music and art appreciation, and famous historical events are often available or even required. Not only that, a study of the local *TV Guide* will unearth many commercial programs which the teacher will want students to view at home; these can teach a great deal as well as entertain, and they rely on impact of the visual and oral image.

The teacher's problem lies not only in knowing specifically what is available, but also in preparing the class for exposure to it and in following up after to see that the learnings are firmed up and retained. In other words, use of the newer educational media should be preceded by discussion, raising questions, sometimes even an assignment, setting the framework into which the new learning can fit. Then it must be followed by answering those questions, clarifying points for individuals, helping students fit it into their total learning pattern, and raising new questions to explore. It is not enough to expose the learner to the educational medium; he must actively fit the learning into his own pattern of interests and needs.

SENSORY MODALITY

We once thought that each of us had some one predominant or preferred sensory avenue of learning, that some of us tend to visualize all stimuli, others to think in terms of what we hear, still others in terms of feeling or movement. Even if people fall into "sensory types," however, it still does not follow that the best condition for learning is through appealing to the preferred sensory mode. Evidence accumulates that what we learn depends, not upon what the stimulus is, but rather upon the response we make to it. Let us examine the concept, however, and see what information useful to teachers may be present in it.

Look at the following list of words. After each one record "V" if the first association is visual in nature, "A" if it is auditory, "M" if it is motor or large-muscle, "T" if it is tactile, and "O" if it is olfactory.

desk	song	sky
horn	knife blade	picture
walk	smoke	splash
bakery	swing	ice
rocking chair	oven	honeysuckle

People usually think of visual associations for *desk, sky,* and *picture;* auditory for *horn, song,* and *splash;* motor for *walk, rocking chair,* and *swing;* tactile for *knifeblade, oven,* and *ice;* and olfactory for *bakery, smoke,* and *honeysuckle.* The chances are that you chose some of each of the letters indicated, showing that responses are mixed in sensory type.

Or compare the following two methods of presenting pseudohistorical material.[1] First of all, read the following selection through once. There will be a brief test on it.

The discovery of Feddah Land was the occasion of many interesting adventures. Captain Betler, who was in command of the ship, approached the land from the east following the strong currents which set in that direction. Starting in the reign of Peter VI, A.D. 1560, from Kenda Town on the Island of Fauly, the explorers had sailed for some days in dangerous seas, and eventually reached the mainland of Feddah with some difficulty. The place at first seemed almost uninhabitable, little being discovered in the way of food. Eventually the party of discovery established their base at a spot they named Erman, situated between two huge promontories. Thence they started into the interior, taking with them rations for thirty days which they had brought from the ship. They had not gone many days directly inland when Captain Betler found that a sharp turn towards the north was necessary, to avoid the huge volcano (called by them Aurora, after the ship). Nestling under the lee of this mighty mountain they

---

[1] Adapted from C. W. Valentine, *An Introduction to Experimental Psychology in Relation to Education.* Boston, Warwick and York, 1916.

discovered a charming glen where they made their second depot, named Densar.

Now take the test below. Check the answers with the text, and record the number right.

Test 1

1. What was the name of the land they discovered?
2. From what direction did they approach the land?
3. How was this direction determined?
4. From what town did they start on their voyage?
5. Where was this town situated?
6. What was their first base?
7. In what direction did they have to turn after going inland?
8. What was the name of the second depot?

Now read *aloud* the second selection at about the same rate, *saying each word aloud* and *tracing the route of the expedition on the map.*

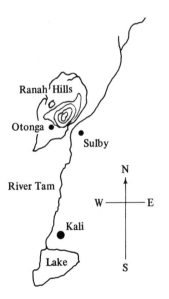

In the first year of the reign of William X of Zamboo, A.D. 2100, a revolt occurred among his subjects living among the hills of Ranah. In these almost inaccessible heights the king's civilized troops at first could do little to suppress the revolt. Eventually, however, the greatest leader of the day, General Wodam, took command of an army, and set out with a large force northwards from Kali on the River Tam. This river flows near the base of the highest hills in the Ranah range, and its valley formed an excellent route for the march. At Sulby, near the hills, they were surprised to find a large band of rebels holding the pass up to the mountain villages. General Wodam, however, leaving a force of 500 men to hold the enemy in check at Sulby, secretly accomplished a forced march towards the southwest and around the hills, and thus captured Otonga, the principal village of the rebels.

Now take the following test. Check with the text above and record the number right.

Test 2

1. What was the place where the rebellion occurred?
2. From what town did the expedition start?
3. Where was that town situated?
4. In which direction did the expedition start?
5. How was the route determined?
6. Where did they find the first rebels?
7. In what direction did the general then march?
8. What was the name of the place eventually captured?

It is probable you had more answers right on the second test than on the first. The major difference between the two is that in the second selection hearing, articulation, and tracing were added to the visual stimulus. There is strong indication that tracing, or the addition of overt muscular activity, increases the permanent effectiveness of learning.

From studies such as these certain principles emerge:

1. *There is no systematic superiority of one sense over others.* Correlations among abilities to learn through all senses are high and positive. Visualization seems to require the greatest degree of mental maturity. Auditory learning or listening is an easier avenue for the younger children. To say that auditory or visual or kinesthetic or vocimotor or manumotor learning is either superior in general or generally superior for any one person is inaccurate. The sensory modality that is superior in a given case depends upon the sense fields available to the subject and the nature of the stimulus presented. Further, whatever the mode of presentation, we translate it into our own preferred imagery, and this is more important than the mode of presentation.

2. *The addition of sensory modalities aids learning.* In general, appealing to two senses is better than to one, to three better than to two. We know that visual and auditory stimulation are superior to either one alone, and that visual-auditory-motor stimulation is superior to visual-auditory. The superiority may be a summation effect, or facilitation, or clarity and certainty of reception. As many sensory approaches as feasible should be used in each learning.

3. *Articulation aids learning.* Oral reading seems to be superior to silent reading for memorizing, though there is a high correlation

between the two. Silent reading involves only visual stimulation, while oral reading involves articulation and hearing as well. Perhaps these additional stimulations explain why we resort to reading aloud under stress. Studies of learning spelling by studying aloud as opposed to studying silently are inconclusive, but we do know that writing words and learning to hear them accurately add to the ability to spell. Articulation is an aid in learning on which we call when the learning is difficult.

4. *Learning with overt movement is superior to purely ideational learning.* This difference is particularly apparent in retention. In immediate learning, the making of the overt movement may require added time but the learning is superior in the long run. Comparisons of typing with code substitution show that typing, by virtue of the larger amount of overt muscular activity, is superior in respect to retention. The value of kinesthetic factors in presenting material is greater for long-term retention than for immediate learning. Imaginary practice produces less improvement than actual practice. Actual movement facilitates learning, particularly when judged by retention.

5. *Patterned visual material aids learning.* It is easier to understand pictures, graphs, and maps than straight textual material. This preference applies especially to immediate learning. Numbers written out in text are harder to remember than Arabic numerals. It is still easier to remember them as round numbers, even easier as graphic comparisons or maps, and still easier as motion pictures developing the comparisons. Within a given sensory modality, then, the degree of patterning of the material is a factor in learning.

6. *Individual differences in learning are present in modality of presentation.* Which sensory appeal will be superior depends upon the nature of the stimulus, the accustomed sensory approach of the individual to that kind of stimulus, his sensory acuity, his mental maturity, and the pleasantness or unpleasantness of the material.

. . . IN THE CLASSROOM

Implications for teaching method are varied and significant, particularly for teaching in remedial and problem areas. The importance of movement and touch and real experience were the basis of much of the work of Rousseau, later that of Itard with the mentally retarded and that of Montessori with slum children. Today similar sensory involvement is basic to methods with children who have minimal cerebral dysfunction, such as those of Frostig and Kephart. Most recently, the research suggestion that children in socially deprived areas have a more "motoric" style of learning has led to trying procedures which include more kinesthetic involvement in teaching that group.

The kinesthetic method of teaching nonreaders consists essentially of reinforcing the usual visual-auditory method by writing the words to be learned. In the beginning stages, the child is asked what he would like to write about. The first word is written for him on the board large enough for him to trace it freely with his index and middle finger (so that the hand is in normal writing position). He traces the word from beginning to end (gaining an impression of it as a whole), saying the word as he traces it (auditory and kinesthetic impression added to visual), until he thinks he can write it correctly. He then tries it at the board, goes back to his pattern if he fails, or writes it in his story if he succeeds. Later on he reads from books, but each time he finds a word he does not recognize he studies it by underlining each syllable as he says it (adding auditory to visual stimulation) and by writing the word (kinesthetic or motor appeal). Such words are reviewed by rereading or in list form or both.

The same principle applies to learning spelling or penmanship. In fact, it applies also to learning foreign languages and symbolic languages such as shorthand. Writing, seeing, and hearing should all proceed concurrently in order to reinforce each other in learning. In teaching spelling, the teacher should encourage the learner to say and to write the words he is spelling. She should check the accuracy of his pronunciation, since the auditory and articulatory appeals are important additions to the visual; studies show as high as twenty percent of spelling errors in upper grades can be avoided by teaching careful pronunciation first. In learning Morse code, sending with the buzzer sound present results in faster learning than sending with the sound unheard by the sender.

In teaching the deaf who are also blind, a special problem occurs. There, learning occurs through touching the teacher's lips and throat, and trying to translate the sensations directly into motor patterns in the student's own vocal organs. With the deaf who retain their sight, lip reading substitutes seeing for hearing; but lip reading is about twenty percent more effective when the words are spoken aloud in spite of the fact that the learner cannot hear them as speech. The vibrotactile sensations from speech, which we do not need when we can hear, are used by the deaf to reinforce the visual stimulus in lip reading.

Even in presenting films, the teacher should supplement films with discussion, thus eliciting articulation and expression. Presenting the film is not enough: the teacher should know film content thoroughly before using it, make the purpose in showing it clear to the class, have the class discuss the film immediately after it is shown, sometimes check the discussion by rerunning the film, and help the students integrate into their own work what they have learned from the film.

An illustration of the use of a number of sensory modalities is reported by a student observer.

After the children thought the problems (arithmetic) out "in their heads," the answers were explained verbally; then sticks were used to allow for kinesthetic appeal. The teacher showed the group how they could arrive at the answer by counting the change that was given back in the form of pennies, pennies and nickels, or pennies and dimes; circles were drawn to represent the coins. Lastly the problem was written as a regular subtraction problem with the numerals under one another.

A classroom situation reported by a student observer exemplifies the use of the pictorial approach as an aid to learning.

The teacher used a picture map to stimulate the students to think out the solution to the problem. The problem stated that Bob was going from one house to another. The total distance was 8.7 miles. At 5.6 miles his bicycle had a flat tire. How far would he have to walk if he did not fix the tire? She asked the children if they would rather walk that distance or get the bicycle fixed.

ACTIVITY: INCIDENTAL MEMORY, INTENT TO REMEMBER, LATENT LEARNING

Now we come to the question of whether we remember whatever is presented to us, or whether we must consciously try to remember in order to learn. We have touched on this matter before in talking about attention and distraction, but more complete analysis will show the importance of activity or reaction on the part of the learner. Essentially, the question is whether the child remembers what is presented to him, or remembers his own response to what is presented. The distinction is an important one.

Take a blank sheet of paper and without measuring draw (1) circles the size of a quarter, dime, nickel, penny, and half dollar; (2) the design on the face of a dollar bill, and (3) an ordinary six-cent postage stamp. Then compare the drawings with the articles. They will be quite incomplete in detail, and even the relative sizes of the coins may be small for the nickel and large for the half dollar.

Research directed toward whether it is necessary to intend to recall when you learn is varied and diverse. From such studies as these we find:

1. *There is little learning without motivation,* or learning that is completely "incidental." Placing an individual in a certain perceptual environment does not guarantee he will perceive. Unless he perceives he will not understand, nor react, nor learn.

2. *Even when he is not instructed to learn, however, the individual often responds to various forms of self-instruction.* His own sets, interests, habitual modes of attack, and more conscious forms of intent provide motivation that makes varied and sporadic forms of learning occur in the absence of external motivation. Sometimes hidden gains, often referred to as latent learning, surface later. The learner himself need not be aware of his motivations or that he is learning or of the component acts of that learning: in other words, it is not essential that he consciously intend to learn. But it is essential that some motivation be operative, even if it is only a tendency to try to understand. Without instruction, what a person learns varies with his point of view and his self-instruction.

3. *The more active the attitude the more effective the learning will be.* Recall in the waking state is superior to recall in the hypnotic trance for all materials except those which have been repressed. Reading material aloud with the knowledge that you will be expected to reproduce it is more effective than simply reading it for someone else's information. Reading under instruction to give special attention to certain parts results in better learning of those parts. Reading to recall at a certain time produces better recall if the question is asked at the time specified than if it is asked either earlier or later than expected. A realistic understanding of the ways in which the information to be learned will be used and when it will be needed is a distinct aid in learning given material.

4. *Any learning that is to be clearly mastered should occupy the*

center of attention for a time. We have an area of attention which may be described as focal, or near the focus, in which we clearly perceive all related materials. Around the focal area is a band of peripheral attention which is less clear, and in which there is perception only as the materials are related to the focus or as they attract attention through some form of self-instruction. Beyond the peripheral area is a zone of nonattention. Any skill that is to be effectively mastered must move into the focal area of attention for a short time. It may first be encountered in a broad context, in the peripheral area as part of a major unit of work; but attention must be shifted to it for intensive work. Then it may be returned to the peripheral area for use in various contexts.

5. *The child's reaction in learning should be accurate.* In the learning situation, it is essential that the child's first experience with a new concept or process be correct, due to the fact that first reactions tend to be the best-remembered. If initial reactions are not checked and (when necessary) corrected, an incorrect impression may be reinforced and remembered. It is much more difficult to rectify an incorrect initial learning and substitute the right response than to make sure the initial response is correct.

6. *Individual differences are greater in incidental learning than in directed learning.* Young children seem to learn more adequately than older children through nondirected forms of attention, perhaps because of less experience, perhaps because of less ability to focus attention when it is requested. Further, the same individual differs from situation to situation in the amount he learns without specific instruction. The amount of practice he has had in such learning also affects the amount of his learning.

. . . IN THE CLASSROOM

These facts again point out the importance of motivation in learning and the relative ineffectiveness of undirected attention. They suggest that the teacher will do two things. She will rely chiefly on helping the learner to explore the material and formulate conscious purposes, making sure that he knows what he wishes to learn and how and when he will use what he learns. She will also, however, have in the environment inviting books, bulletin-board displays, and objects which will catch self-directed attention. These peripheral materials will add to and enrich the experience of some individuals in the class.

The facts also stress the importance of an active, problem-solving attitude on the part of the learner. He is not a passive being, manipulated by the teacher to produce learning; rather, he must be the active agent if effective learning is to occur. An expectant, alert attitude and a conscious purpose in learning result in more rapid progress than a desultory approach. The teacher can produce an expectant attitude by setting conditions within the classroom that will capture attention before formal learning begins.

The relation of the context to the teaching of skills is of special importance. Skills should be introduced in the context in which they will be used in order to give them meaning. If a skill is to be mastered, it must also be lifted momentarily from that context and the focus of attention put on the specific word or process or symbol so that it may be clearly learned. Then it should again be returned to context and used there. For example, a child learning to spell asks for help with a word he does not know; the teacher shows him how to write it and he studies it until he can reproduce it correctly; then he goes on with his writing. Later, in a special spelling period he is given the same word, asked to recall the sentence in which he used it, and allowed to practice writing it several times.

Just how to manage the details of such a complex procedure in teaching spelling sometimes puzzles teachers. One supervisor suggests:

> To begin with, each student should have his own "spelling book," in which will be written all the words he is supposed to learn to spell. They may come from the weekly list of words which is given to the class, or they may come from his other papers, or from the stories he writes for the language period.
>
> When a spelling test is given, the student hands in his paper inside the spelling book. The teacher writes in his spelling book the words he misspelled, or as many of them as she thinks he will be able to learn during the week. Similarly, every time he turns in a story or comes to her for criticism before copying it, he brings his spelling book along and she enters in it words for him to study.
>
> Each student then has his own spelling list, tailored to fit his own needs. His teacher has taught him to study spelling by underlining the syllables, saying the word meanwhile, until he thinks he can write it. Then he tries to write it, and checks his spelling by underlining syllables as he compares it with the model. If it is wrong he studies again. If it is right, he turns over his paper (to prevent piecemeal copying) and writes it three times, each time covering the word above with his hand.
>
> When he thinks he knows all his words, he turns to his "spelling part-

ner" and asks that he dictate the words. His teacher then checks his book from time to time to see how he is progressing.

The important features are that each child has his own list of words selected in terms of difficulty for him, and drawn from a context in which he has personally met them. The work load is kept down so that he can handle it successfully, and students are encouraged to work together. It really isn't so difficult to handle. The increased interest and efficiency more than compensate for the complexity.

Similarly, the child learning a word first encounters it in context. He figures out what it means, or asks the teacher, or (in upper grades) looks it up in a dictionary and records it in his word book. Later he is given practice on his new words or phrases. In arithmetic, when he needs to add two numbers he first uses concrete objects; then the teacher shows him how the same problem would look written in numbers; and still later he masters that particular number combination. Constant interweaving between context and isolation of the skill is an important part of teaching technique.

ACTIVITY: THE READING-RECITATION PROCESS

Now we come to the question of how an active attitude on the part of the learner can be stimulated as well as how effective that attitude is in creating more favorable conditions for learning. How much time shall we spend in demonstration? How much talking should we do, and how much draw from the learner? Do we learn when we are passive?

Much of the pertinent experimentation is concerned with the effect of introducing attempts at recall during the reading or study of the material. Perhaps the nature of the problem will become clearer from an experience in learning two verses. Read silently, three times, the following verse from Burns's "Address to the Unco Guid." Read it straight through each time.

> Then gently scan your brother man,
>> Still gentler sister woman;
> Tho' they may gang a kennin wrang,
>> To step aside is human:
> One point must still be greatly dark,
>> The moving *Why* they do it;
> And just as lamely can ye mark,
>> How far perhaps they rue it.

Take a sheet of blank paper and write as much of the verse as possible. Score it, giving one point for each word correct and in correct order.

Now read silently, once, the following verse from the same source:

> Who made the heart, 'tis He alone
>> Decidedly can try us;
> He knows each chord, its various tone,
>> Each spring, its various bias;
> Then at the balance let's be mute,
>> We never can adjust it;
> What's done we partly may compute,
>> But not know what's resisted.

On a sheet of blank paper write as much of the verse as possible. Then read it a second time; again write it. Then read it a third time and write it. Score the *third* trial by giving one point for each word correct and in correct order.

Now compare the two records. There were probably more words right on the second verse because of the more active attitude generated by attempted recall between readings. Attempted recall aids in learning.

Research studies include laboratory experiments and studies of classroom procedures. In general such studies show:

1. *The more active the participation of the learner, the more effective the learning.* Attempted recall or recall with self-prompting results in better learning than simply rereading the same material. Re-presentation without recall is consistently ineffective, particularly in retention.

Reading followed by taking a test results in more learning than covering the same material without test. The attempted recall aids learning. Written examinations are more effective than oral because of the more intensive use of the time of each individual.

Laboratory experimentation is superior to lecture-demonstration in effectiveness. Lecture-demonstration is superior to discussion or lecture-discussion for college and high-school students. Discussion is superior to lecture; and lecture is superior to reading for the average student. This order holds true for facts gained, understanding of principles, and resourcefulness in problem solving. The greater the degree of student activity, the more the learning.

Note taking aids recall because the student does something about what he hears. The more clear, full, and definite his notes, the more gain there is from note taking. Verbatim notes are less helpful than summaries. Being on the alert for information, asking questions, taking tests, and marking one's own paper all produce better learning than listening passively to what is presented.

Amount of effort is positively related to the amount learned and retained. In addition, the individual who participates actively develops greater interest in what he is learning even though his grades may not improve. All these findings point up the fact that we learn and recall only that to which we respond and in the degree to which we respond. We do not remember the stimulus but rather what we did in response to the stimulus.

2. *The greater the proportion of time given to active response, the greater the learning.* The limit is that the initial presentation must be long enough for full presentation of the "whole"; it must permit giving the outline of what is to be learned. Within that limit, the earlier attempted recall is introduced and the more frequently it is used, the more effective the learning.

3. *Individual differences occur in the effectiveness of overt activity in learning.* Young children gain more from activity and attempted recall than older, and their activity is essentially overt rather than symbolic or mental. They have fewer concepts with which to work and possess a shorter attention span. Similarly, bright students can work more easily with symbols, and can learn more easily from reading and lecture. Activity is especially helpful in the learning of material that is essentially meaningless and unconnected, since there are fewer other cues to aid in learning.

Essentially, then, we learn through what we do and not through what is done to us. We remember our own responses, not the stimuli. Students are more willing to part with their texts than with their term papers when time for housecleaning arrives. The axiom that we love people less for the good they have done us than for the good we have done them is a statement of the same principle. Interest in manipulation or in activity seems to be a basic human tendency, and the teaching which takes that tendency into consideration is more effective than that which considers learning to be a passive assimilative process.

. . . IN THE CLASSROOM

All these findings suggest that provision for student reaction is an essential part of every learning situation. When an arithmetic process is presented, the learning is not complete until the student has had a chance to do some problems himself. In planning for units of work, the learner should become involved in planning and executing the activities, and take the initiative insofar as he can. Studies of the popularity of school subjects show that opportunities for bodily activity, discussion, and argument are strong factors in creating interest. The experienced story teller gives children an opportunity to guess what is coming next or to devise their own endings. In building vocabulary, the teacher encourages students to note new words learned and to do something with each new word and thus emphasize the learning.

An example of the effective use of activity is reported by a student observer:

> In the first part of the arithmetic lesson the children were making yeast dough. The children first read the reading chart telling the amount of the ingredients. The teacher said, "When Mary is through measuring the flour, she will hold up the cup for you to see if she measured correctly." She held it up and the class approved. She then asked, "How much water should we use?" There were various answers. She said, "If we filled up one-third of the cup, how many thirds would be left?" The class gave the correct answer.

> She then asked the class (tipping the bowl so children could see), if one-third cup of water mixed up that much dough, how much more they would need to mix it all up. The children were allowed to experiment until they had enough water in the ingredients to make it a stiff dough.

> After the dough was mixed she asked them what they should do now. They looked for a suitable spot in which to place it. By questions of this sort the children's minds were stimulated to solve the problem of the yeast dough themselves.

Conversely, the teacher tries to avoid having the learner invest energy or activity in finding answers which are distinctly wrong. The teacher of reading in primary grades must often decide whether to tell the child a word or to encourage him to work it out. Word recognition is not a matter of problem solving but one in which, no matter what the child thinks, the true answer remains fixed. To press him too far in working out a word so that he guesses, and probably gets a wrong answer, means that the wrong answer is fixed in his memory. He will remember his guess rather than the teacher's correction because it is *his*. Instead, the right word should be given to him as soon as it is apparent that he is genuinely confused. The same thing holds true for calling attention to errors in such situations.

Similarly, the teacher who gives the student homework in an area with which he is having difficulty on the assumption that he needs extra practice is on dangerous ground. The chances are that the learner will be unable to do the work alone. His parent will show him how to do it, perhaps by a different method. The parent will demonstrate again and again. The student will still not understand because he has only watched the work. The net result is that it is the *parent*, not the student, who learns how to do the homework.

In all these situations, then, it is well to remember that the student learns through his own reactions and not through what is presented to him. Activity on the part of the learner results in fixing whatever his responses were, whether right or wrong.

ACTIVITY: DEGREE OF GUIDANCE

The teacher must decide, too, when to help a student and when to let him work out a problem for himself, when to answer a question and when to lead him to find his own answers, and when to give no answer at all. In psychological terms, we are speaking of "degree of guidance." This scientific use of the term is to be distinguished from the common use of the term in schools. Here we refer simply to how much initiative should rest with the child. Many well-meaning adults assume that they should provide maximum stimulation and give answers to all questions that arise. They take it for granted that, because they have given an answer, the child will learn it. Others claim that only what the individual discovers for himself is important to him. The teacher must often reach a balance between these two positions.

Research in this field shows a reasonably high degree of agreement. From such studies we seem to find:

1. *Either too little or too much guidance is ineffective.* There is an intermediate point at which the optimal amount of guidance is reached. With progressively increasing amounts of guidance, learning becomes increasingly effective to a certain point, then decreases. Help results in gain at first, then becomes detrimental if it is too long continued. Guidance at all points seems to affect speed more than it affects ultimate mastery.

The effect of too little guidance is that there is little growth or that the child becomes discouraged and moves away from the learning problem. The effect of too much guidance is even worse, especially when it is given late in the process of mastering a specific skill. Too much guidance results in increased variability, less effectiveness in learning, and less transfer. The learner seems to react as he does to dominance by developing active resistance to learning. The best learning occurs if guidance is given in small amounts, that is, if the learner discovers or seems to discover the answers for himself instead of having the right answers given to him.

2. *The best timing for guidance is early in the development of a new skill.* Relatively great amounts of initial guidance can be effective, as in demonstrating a new skill or tracing a new word for writing or formulating questions to be answered in a reading period. Some opportunity should be given at first to explore the material. Then the teacher may well suggest a short, concrete, easily remembered rule of action. It is important that the suggestion be made *when the learner feels the need for help.* Guidance may be detrimental when given at the wrong stage of action.

3. *Guidance is most effectively given in symbolic form.* Even when the teacher shows the child how to do something, the learner should remain the active agent in learning. If she tells him what to do, or uses verbal guidance, he must still translate the idea into action, and learn through the translation. If she demonstrates because words do not communicate effectively at his learning level, she should let him make a maximum number of suggestions and give directions. She may ask him to describe the process as she does it, then let him tell her what to do, then do it himself.

If guidance must be manual, as in tracing, the learner moves his own hand as the teacher watches and tells him what to do. The teacher does not hold his hand and move it for him. Because it is so often passive, manual guidance is usually ineffective, sometimes even detrimental to learning, with human beings. Demonstration is usually superior to manual guidance for young children, and verbal guidance to demonstration for older and brighter students. The value in each case lies in the fact that guidance is symbolic and the learner retains the initiative in doing the act.

Guidance is best used to call attention to significant aspects of the problem and to suggest generalizations, followed by practice of the skill. With guidance used in this way, there is transfer because the same generalizations apply under other conditions, the child understands what they mean, and he has practice in applying them.

4. *Guidance is best given in positive form.* The studies of emphasis on right and wrong responses, referred to in the section of knowledge of results, also stressed this point. Stressing errors is superior to no guidance at all, so long as the learner retains the initiative, but correct guidance is better still. In teaching skills where there is only one correct response (as in spelling) it is important to avoid emphasizing errors, as we have already pointed out. But where there are several relatively good and relatively poor ways of reaching the same objective, as in science or social studies or procedures in handling materials, the learner should have freedom to try out his own methods of solution. The important thing is to let the student retain the initiative, making suggestions at appropriate points, and to let him follow through the procedures he wants to try even if they seem poor to us. Then, if he fails, the teacher can overlook his error and again make a positive suggestion.

. . . IN THE CLASSROOM

In the material on guidance we have additional evidence that the learner must maintain an active attitude and carry the initiative in learning. The teacher can decide when to help and when not to help by observing whether the motivation is lagging, by asking a pertinent question to direct his effort, and by judging whether the problem is too complex for the individual's learning level. In a sense, the position of the Roman tutor in relation to the child on the way to school is symbolic of the modern teacher's psychological relationship to the learner. The tutor walked to one side, a step behind the child, carrying the learning materials and books and protecting him from harm. Similarly, the teacher lets the learner lead the way in devising objectives and procedures, feeds him material and suggestions as they are pertinent, and sees that he ultimately reaches his goal.

A pertinent incident was noted by a student observer.

The class was working on a unit on the harbor, and many children were trying to make small boats from blocks with pieces inserted for masts.

One small boy was having great difficulty with his drill. He tried several positions, and eventually settled on holding the drill up with the wood balanced on top of it, drilling through from the bottom.

The teacher noticed him and came over. She said, "If you would put the wood down on the saw horse and drill through from above it would be easier."

His answer, with no intention of impertinence, was "You do it your way, and I'll do it mine."

A little later, when he had tried out his way and found out just how difficult it was, the teacher found him drilling her way.

The teacher should either have reached him before he started his own method or have waited until he had fully explored his wrong way and was ready to try a different one.

We know how useless it is to try to teach a young child to walk by putting him through the movements. Instead, when he is standing and pulling himself around by holding to furniture, we hold out a favorite toy or a bit of food; and he walks suddenly under his own power. In teaching a child to write, it is of little help to put his hand through the correct movements. Instead we provide a model, show him how to trace it, let him trace it, let him trace several times, then write it by himself. In teaching a friend to ride a bicycle we do better to choose a soft lawn, help the learner mount, give him a push, and let go. Trying to run alongside, hold him up, and shout instructions is not helpful. Or, as in the case of the small boy and the drill, it is better to let the child work out the matter in his own way instead of taking away the material and tools to avoid a mistake.

PROBLEM SOLVING

Problem solving is a favorite term in modern education. Sometimes we have the impression that it is a kind of learning set apart, a completely different way of approaching the learning process. Actually, it is essentially a form of learning in which the initiative in discovering answers rests chiefly with the learner, in contrast to forms in which the teacher demonstrates facts and the student assimilates. In this sense, problem solving is related to the principle of activity and especially to guidance. It is the situation in which the learner's initiative is at a maximum.

There have been direct studies of the nature of the process of problem solving, some with particular stress on the function of insight, and some on age differences in ability to solve problems. The studies of the process of problem solving seem to show:

1. *The problem to be solved must be adapted to the perceptual level of the learner.* Though this requirement is important in all learning, it is most essential here since the essence of problem solving is self-direction and discovery. Problem solving is a process of forming concepts from perceptions, of taking the thinglike impression and building it to an idea. It is the process of inductive reasoning. The concept must not be too taxing, and it should be relatively close to the perceptual level of the learner. The nature of percepts and the breadth of gap from percept to concept which the individual can bridge are functions of the age and degree of mental maturity of the learner. Problem solving has its greatest advantage in retention. It more often transfers to new learnings than do other forms of instruction.

2. *In problem solving, some initial exploration and manipulation are necessary.* How much is needed depends upon how much experience the individual can already bring to bear on the problem. The initial exploration involves clarification of the problem and its surrounding conditions. It is not trial-and-error learning in the sense in which that term is usually understood, but it is better described as exploration and clarification.

3. *Finding a directional cue after the initial exploration aids problem solving.* The cue results in a reorganization of the perceptual field in terms of that cue, hence in changing the relationships between facts and meanings, and therefore the perception of the facts. Sometimes the cue comes from a carefully worded question of the teacher. If so, the teacher must be careful not to give too much help, for giving the answer or demonstrating is actually detrimental to problem solving. The learner must retain the psychological initiative. Sometimes the cue comes from what has been called the atmosphere effect, or the direction in which the facts the student has explored seem to point. Whatever the origin of the "schema," the learner then directs his thinking toward it, explores, evaluates, and analyzes it.

4. *Eventually insight occurs.* Insight is characterized by its non-overt nature. It is a reorganization of the field, often unconscious. Because it is sudden and unconscious does not mean that there is anything mystic about the process. It simply means that the learner has enough percepts near the concept so that the concept easily and naturally falls into place to complete the structure. Insight is often contrasted with trial-and-error learning because the external mani-

festations are quite different. They are really two extremes of the same continuum, from the learning that seems to occur quickly and without overt or conscious activity to the learning that is long and laborious with much overt activity.

. . . in the Classroom

How difficult it is to keep the middle ground between saying "That is *your* problem" and simply giving the answer is illustrated in the case of the two boys who were building the platform described previously. There the teacher had given too little guidance, simply telling them to use a ruler. They did not know that a ruler is divided into twelve inches, and that twelve inches and six inches make eighteen inches. So they left the task and discharged energy in rough-housing.

The teacher, pressed for time, might have made the opposite mistake of saying, "Bring me your ruler. Measure one full ruler length and mark it, then measure six more inches from that mark." That direction would solve the immediate problem but would result in little permanent or transferable learning. Her best procedure would have been to ask the boys to wait a moment if she was in the midst of something else, and then say, "You see those marks across the ruler? They are inches. How many of them are there? Now if you start from twelve and count again until you come to eighteen, how many more inches will you need? How will you go about getting eighteen inches, then?" In other words, giving just enough help so that the child can figure the rest out for himself stimulates a deeper insight.

There are many things that the teacher can do to aid in the process of problem solving, though the major initiative must always rest with the learner. She can increase the student's awareness of problems through field trips and exhibits and questioning. She can aid him in clarifying the problem and exploring its conditions by providing information and experiences, showing him how to use the library, to skim, to read, and to take notes. She can help him define the problem adequately by guiding him to withhold judgment, explore thoroughly, and organize his work systematically, and by staving off action until he has fully explored and systematized his knowledge. She can help him to discover cues or hypotheses by providing added experiences, reducing the problem to its simplest form, giving hints and suggestions, and encouraging him to drop the problem for the moment when he seems blocked. She can help him to evaluate his hypotheses by fostering "if—then" thinking or rational analysis of cause and effect, by teaching him how to form deductions by logical reasoning, by gaining his willingness to reason and to withhold action and judgment until his reasoning is complete, and by helping him to admit that sometimes he simply does not have enough evidence to solve the problem. It is evident in all this that the skills and attitudes the child is learning extend far beyond the specific task on which he is working.

IMPLICATIONS

From all of these principles, the following suggestions for teachers seem justified:

1. Try to make each impression vivid. Use contrast in relative size. Use color contrast. Use movement and development. Vary the procedure to retain novelty.

2. Present material through as many sensory modalities as you can. Encourage the learner to speak as he learns whenever it is appropriate. Encourage manipulation of materials for kinesthetic and motor impression. Encourage the student to move about as he learns. Use pictures, graphs, and maps to help him visualize what he is learning.

3. Help the learner to maintain an active attitude at all times. Define the purposes before the learning starts. Stress learning for permanent retention and for use. Isolate for attention any important specific learning.

4. Provide for reaction on the part of the learner in every learning situation. Stress discussion, attempted recall, note taking, questioning. Avoid lecturing, reading, and too much demonstration. Avoid situations that lead to guessing.

5. Provide just enough help to keep the learner moving ahead. Give help as soon as it is needed. Give most of the help early in the learning. Give help in a form that requires action on the part of the learner. Avoid helping too much, too late, or when the student is busy with his own attempt. Give help in positive rather than negative form.

6. Encourage the learner to solve problems for himself. Encourage him to explore the problem freely at first. Give him cues for

solution through questions or experiences, not through statements or demonstrations. Stress skills, attitudes, and processes that will transfer to other problem-solving situations.

EXERCISES IN APPLICATION

1. College students usually keep their term papers for a longer period of time than they do their lecture notes. Why? What learning principle does this preference illustrate?

2. In an experiment with mentally retarded children the "manual tracing" and the "sight" methods were compared. Retention was distinctly better when manual tracing was used. Does this result mean that all children should learn through manual tracing? Why was manual tracing better for this group?

3. Analyze laboratory experimentation, lecture-demonstration, and reading as methods of teaching science in the high school. Which is most effective? Why? Are there limits or qualifications to the use of even the most effective method?

4. Suppose that it takes you half of your study time to read the chapter assigned. Is it best to use the remaining time in rereading, attempting to outline the chapter from memory, resting, going to another assignment, or what? What principle is operating?

5. Mme. Guireaux likes to use each Friday for oral review of the French vocabulary introduced during that week. Mlle. Poirot, instead, gives a ten-minute written test on the day's vocabulary each day. Other things being equal, in which class will the vocabulary scores at mid term be higher? What factors are operating in the two procedures?

6. In presenting a relatively simple new process in arithmetic, Teacher L worked each of six problems through at the board, explaining as she went what she was doing. Teacher M presented the same process by working one problem through and explaining it, having the class tell her what to do on a second, then having each student work through the four others at their seats with one student working at the board for checking. Which class will have mastered the process better at the end of the period? Which will recall better the next day? What principle is functioning?

7. In teaching a child to read, various methods are used including the use of charts and books, reading aloud and being read to, and having the child write and read and illustrate his own stories. Which would you expect to be most effective with a child who is having difficulty in reading? Why?

8. Suppose you are teaching a nine-year-old boy who has just arrived from São Paulo to hit a baseball. He speaks little English. How will you go about teaching him? By putting his hands on the bat and letting him feel

the swing or by demonstrating with another bat? By demonstrating and getting perfect form before a ball is pitched to him, or by just letting him try and correcting errors, or what? What learning concept governs your decision?

9. In which case will class attention be higher, one in which each student reads aloud a part of a common assignment or one in which each student reads a story he has written himself? Under what conditions will the teacher use oral reading in the first grade? In the sixth grade?

10. How can the teacher aid a student in clarifying a problem and exploring its conditions? What types of experiences will help? How can a teacher help him evaluate his hypothesis?

SUGGESTIONS FOR FURTHER READING

Ausubel, D. D. "Cognitive Structure and the Facilitation of Meaningful Verbal Learning." *J. Teach. Educ., 14,* 217–222, 1963. A theoretical paper pointing out differences between rote and logical learning, the importance of clear sequence, and the importance of step-by-step mastery in building meaningful organization.

Corman, B. R. "Learning: II. Problem Solving and Related Topics." *Rev. Educ. Res., 28,* 459–467, 1958. A review of studies of problem solving in relation to attributes of the learner, the experimental design, and the process of learning.

Davis, Gary A. "Current Status of Research and Theory in Human Problem Solving." *Psych. Bull., 66,* 36–54, 1966. An analysis of the process of problem solving from the point of view of traditional learning theory, cognitive theory, and computer and mathematical models.

Edling, J. V. "Instructional Technology and Research." *J. Teach. Educ., 13;* 346–353, 1962. An analysis of six elements in teaching with emphasis on instructional stimuli and newer educational media.

Gallagher, J. J. "Meaningful Learning and Retention: Intrapersonal Cognitive Variables." *Rev. Educ. Res., 34,* 499–512, 1964. A three-year review of research emphasizing intellectual structure, creativity, cognitive style, and cognitive growth.

Kleinmutz, Benjamin, ed. *Problem Solving: Research, Method, and Theory.* New York: Wiley, 1966. A collection of papers on cognitive and behavioristic approaches to problem solving.

Lumsdaine, A. A., and A. M. May. "Mass Communication and Educational Media." *Ann. Rev. Psych., 16,* 475–534, 1965. A somewhat technical review of research on the effectiveness of audiovisual methods of instruction, including films, open- and closed-circuit television, and sound tracks.

Magdol, Miriam. "An Historical Perspective to Physiological Education." *Academic Ther. Quart., 3,* 162–170, 1968. A review of the philosophical and historical foundations of teaching the mentally retarded and brain-damaged from Locke, Rousseau, and Montessori to Kephart and Frostig.

Posner, M. I. "Immediate Memory and Sequential Tasks." *Psych. Bull., 60,* 333–349, 1963. A discussion of factors affecting memory for sequential tasks.

Roberts, R., and J. C. Coleman. "An Investigation of Visual and Kinesthetic Factors in Reading Failure." *J. Educ. Res., 51,* 445–451, 1958. A study of the effect of kinesthetic elements in the presentation of new materials to disability cases and normal readers.

Preventing Forgetting

Thus far we have been concerned with how to achieve the highest level of mastery during the process of learning. The first and most important way of assuring that learning is permanent is to make sure the original teaching is effective. If the material is meaningful, is taught logically and vividly and with maximum understanding and learner activity, it will not only be learned easily but also forgotten less rapidly. No amount of special attention to techniques for bolstering the permanence of retention will be effective unless that which is to be retained has been well taught originally.

Given good initial teaching, however, there are several ways of helping to make learning lasting or "permanent." How lasting and how detailed the recall must be, to what extent the recall must be exact, and to what extent it must transfer to new situations will vary with the nature of the learning.

Let us separate the problems of retention into those of transfer and of forgetting. The problems of transfer deal with those conditions where the learning is used in modified or generalized form rather than in the way in which it was originally learned. These problems are concerned with how learning affects new and similar learnings yet to come, either as a reinforcing or as an interfering agent.

In the present chapter we are concerned with the degree of retention of what was originally learned. We are concerned with forgetting, with why it occurs, and with how to prevent it.

155

FORGETTING

The new teacher is often startled by the extent to which skills the children knew at one time are forgotten during, vacations and absences. A first-grade child who is ill for a few weeks seems to have forgotten how to read on his return to school. A fifth-grade teacher finds that her class, on returning from the summer vacation, seems to have forgotten all about fractions and decimals, and she even has some doubt about its capacity to handle division. A graduate student is irritated with himself because he has to learn how to extract square root all over again after having learned it in the eighth grade, in algebra, and in college mathematics. Sometimes it seems that our minds are sievelike, needing constant refilling.

Studies of forgetting are a part of nearly every learning experiment. The length of time required for mastery is measured, then a check for retention over varied periods of time is applied. Usually the amount retained is proportional to the degree of learning, though sometimes differences which are not apparent in immediate learning show up in retention. We will not attempt to review all of those findings, cutting as they do across the whole learning process. Instead we will confine ourselves to a brief consideration of the characteristic learning and forgetting process.

Certain of the general findings from such research will bear emphasis.

1. *Learning conforms rather universally to some part of the S curve.* We saw that when there is little transfer from previous experience we tend to get a slow, gradually accelerating rise in the curve. We also found that in school situations there is a relatively great amount of transfer, and hence we usually find a curve with a rapid initial rise and a slow leveling off. When we find different curve forms they often mean that we are concentrating on different segments of the total learning curve for the process undertaken.

2. *Plateaus represent learning or measurement failures, not essential characteristics of the learning curve.* Plateaus or irregularities often occur in specific curves. They usually represent failure of motivation, failure to measure learning in fine enough units to show what is occurring, or new conditions that have been introduced into the learning situation.

3. *Some forgetting may always be expected, but total forgetting never occurs.* Studies of forgetting in formal subjects over long

periods of time show that roughly one-third of the content learned in high-school courses is retained one year later, and a similar proportion of the content of college courses is retained one to five years later. Specific motor skills are somewhat more permanent. Studies of adult retention show that there is no such thing as permanent learning, but that the degree of forgetting depends upon the functioning of the learned material in the adult life of the individual.

4. *The characteristic forgetting curve shows a rapid initial drop in retention, followed by leveling off.* The level at which the decline stops depends upon a number of factors, chiefly the degree of meaning and the degree of learning. But the rate of loss is always proportionately greater immediately after learning than it is later on. By way of comparison, the characteristic transfer curve shows an initial rise instead of an initial drop.

. . . IN THE CLASSROOM

These facts mean that the teacher should expect some forgetting from day to day and from week to week, and consciously plan to meet the situation where a high level of retention is desirable. Teachers often notice this fact with some shock. A new teacher, going into a sixth grade and expecting to begin the teaching of percentage, found that the class as a whole knew little about decimals, and had even forgotten much of importance about fractions. Since she was new, she assumed that the teaching in the fifth grade had been poor. Later she learned that the fifth-grade teacher was one of the best teachers of arithmetic in the district, and that mid-year transfers from her class were well prepared for advanced work. During the summer months the formal arithmetic processes had simply been forgotten.

First-grade teachers sometimes have an even more trying experience. Children return from a vacation or an illness and appear to have forgotten all that they knew. Words the teacher was sure they could recognize are gone. The teacher is discouraged. But those words come back very quickly with reteaching. One teacher of experience and wisdom estimated that six weeks would be required each fall to bring her class back to the proficiency it had achieved the previous June, and designed her work to meet this need.

In such cases, the factors producing forgetting were particularly strong. But the child who could not recall the words or processes had not entirely forgotten. Even when we have no conscious memory, there is a residue of each experience in our attitudes and behavior sets. That residue influences our subsequent behavior, and aids in relearning what has apparently been forgotten. A student who has once learned to extract square root and can recall none of the process will need much less time to learn it again when necessity requires than is needed for mastery by another who has never learned the process. Perhaps many specific skills need be mastered only to this level.

LEVEL OF RETENTION

Knowing that some forgetting always occurs, we must decide what level of retention we want and how that level of retention can be secured. Sometimes the teacher presents material that is most important in its effect on appreciations; she does not care whether the students remember exactly what was done, but is concerned with broad attitudes. Sometimes she cares greatly whether the student remembers the exact learning, as in the spelling of a word, and wishes to assure retention of the specific skill. She goes about these two types of learning in different ways.

Experimental studies use several different methods of measuring retention, and comparative studies have been made of the level of retention each shows. Sometimes the learner is asked to *recall* what he has learned, that is, to rehearse exactly what was presented to him, as in memorizing poetry or writing spelling words or doing arithmetic problems. Sometimes he is given the correct steps in a process and asked to *recognize* the process, that is, given a list of possible answers to the question and asked to select the right one. Sometime he is not asked for the answers directly, but is given a chance to *relearn* the material and his retention is measured by how much time he saves the second time over the original learning. All of these are methods of measuring the level of retention, but they apply to different degrees of mastery of the material.

In general we find:

1. *Different degrees of retention are measured by recall, recognition, and relearning.* To say that nothing is remembered because nothing can be recalled is a fallacy. We often fail to recall names, but select them from a list. We are unable to spell a word, but we can select the correct spelling from a list of alternatives. The question is not whether but how well we remember.

2. *A learner's ability to recall demonstrates relatively complete retention; ability to recognize, an intermediate amount; and ability to relearn, relatively little.* These differences are illustrated in Figure 5 for three levels of retention. Measurements of recognition and relearning show relatively little loss, while measurements of recall show a greater amount. The difference between the methods is not in the amount retained, but in the effectiveness of the tests of retention used to measure how much was retained.

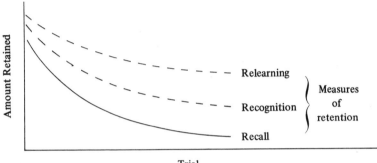

FIGURE 5. FEW LEARNINGS ARE COMPLETELY LOST

The significance of these facts goes far beyond the question of what kind of examinations to use, or how to measure the results of learning. We must decide what level of retention we wish for a particular learning. The easy answer is that everything we do should be "permanently" retained at the highest level, but analysis will show that would be very difficult to attain and probably undesirable. The problem is to differentiate between those learnings which must remain at the level of recall, those which may drop to the level of recognition, and those in which easy relearning is sufficient.

. . . IN THE CLASSROOM

Let us analyze characteristic school learnings from this point of view. In skill fields such as word recognition, spelling, arithmetic facts, and language usage, it is clear that only retention at the level of recall is satisfactory. It is not enough for a student to recognize a correct spelling; he must be able to recall it at will. He must be able to recognize words, and to find the meanings of new words from context and from a dictionary. He must know his arithmetic facts and processes and retain them distinctly so that he can use them without help. Because such skills must be recalled in exact form to be useful, a relatively higher degree of original learning is essential. It is in the teaching of skills that preventing forgetting is most important, because permanent retention at the level of the original learning is essential.

In the content fields, such as social studies, science, and literature, relatively few facts of much that is presented need to be learned to the level of recall. The student need not be able to recall exactly how the pioneers reached the west coast or exactly when Ohio was settled or the names of the members of Lincoln's Cabinet; it is important, rather, that he should recognize places and events and persons as part of an over-all movement of significance to him. He needs the specific facts only as general background. For this reason, extensive drill is out of place in content fields. If the original learning is complete and clear, there is no need to retain the specifics permanently. The normal forgetting process may be allowed to occur.

We need only analyze the adult uses of school learnings to see this use of content. The adult reads newspapers and books. In reading a news event about a famine in India, he must be able to recall the words he reads, but he need only recognize as familiar the fact that India is a thickly populated area using primitive agricultural methods. Most of the places and persons and dates are unimportant to him. In listening to a musical selection, most people's chief reaction is one of enjoyment rather than analysis, and the important recall is perhaps that of the composer and name in case the listener wishes to hear the selection again. Though what we teach in school is important, it is not essential that everything should be recalled permanently in clear and isolated form. We often teach for the sake of providing richness of association or for the sake of enjoyment, not for recall.

Where the stress is on appreciations and attitudes, still less specific recall is needed. The teacher reads a story to the class or plays a musical recording or takes the class on a visit to an art gallery. It is not important for them to remember the story or recording or exhibit, or even to remember they had that particular experience. The important thing is that they should like hearing good stories and music and seeing fine paintings. With such a low level of specific retention needed, drill is unnecessary. Memorization of authors and characters, music-memory contests, and picture-naming drills are unsuitable for the kind of retention that is desired. Such drills result in specific recall rather than in the generalized attitudes that come from diverse and pleasurable experience.

We are saying, then, that the teacher must adjust to her purpose in teaching any particular lesson the extent to which she tries to counteract forgetting. The techniques discussed below are appropriate only if permanent retention at the level of recall is necessary. Overlearning and distribution of practice are concepts applicable chiefly to skills and to rote rather than fully meaningful tasks.

OVERLEARNING

The first technique useful in counteracting forgetting is overlearning or drill. A student who has just learned the meaning of a new word is asked for it in a second and a third context. Or the student practices writing a new spelling word until he gets it right; then his teacher asks him to write it again three more times, just for practice. Students learn how to do a problem in long division, then do a number of similar problems for practice. The teacher's question is how much practice there should be, and how it should be timed.

Research on overlearning is concerned with practice as a condition of learning, and with the effect of various amounts of practice in preventing forgetting. The studies of overlearning seem to indicate that:

1. *Practice is a condition, not a method, of learning.* Practice alone causes no increase in the amount learned; but practice of a response already learned tends to help fix that response. The quality of the practice is what counts. The practice must be on meaningful material already mastered, done with full attention and with a check on accuracy.

2. *Overlearning results in more permanent retention than learning to mastery alone.* There is some increase in retention with each degree of overlearning. Some drill on facts that must be permanently recalled just as they have been presented is distinctly helpful.

3. A little overlearning is proportionately more effective than a great deal. A law of diminishing returns operates as overlearning progresses. In general, about 50 percent overlearning seems profitable for retention. More than 50 percent overlearning is uneconomical for most materials and most time intervals.

The relation between degree of learning and retention is illustrated in Figure 6. When learning is incomplete or barely complete, forgetting is relatively rapid. When overlearning occurs, however, there is little forgetting over long periods of time.

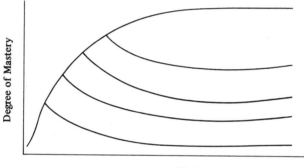

Trials

FIGURE 6. THE MORE COMPLETE THE LEARNING THE LESS THE FORGETTING

. . . IN THE CLASSROOM

Teachers disagree on the extent to which overlearning is needed in the classroom. One supervisor believes:

If we really teach our best, I think drill is unnecessary. If you teach a word or an arithmetic process with enough meaning and vividness, the learner will remember it from just one experience. Give your attention to making the initial teaching effective and you won't need drill.

Besides, to stop to learn to spell a word in the midst of composition interrupts the train of thought. Let the student learn it if he can easily; if not, let him copy it or even misspell it, but don't interrupt him. There will be a time when he can learn to spell it correctly.

If a word is important for a student, it will come up again in new contexts. That is the way spelling lists are built. You don't have to improvise artificial situations for review.

Another supervisor disagrees:

It is true that the more effective the initial teaching, the less drill will be needed. But think of the number of things you remember that you learned only once; they are very few. You can't safely leave drill to chance.

I would agree that you should not interrupt the flow of thought to drill on a word. But it is equally important not to let the student get started on an incorrect spelling. If spelling is such a difficult problem for one individual, let another student who is particularly good in spelling help him, or have only a part of the class doing writing at the same time so that he can have plenty of help, or let him dictate his story to the teacher at the typewriter. But *don't* let him misspell words.

It is true, too, that the word will come up in new contexts, but that is not enough. It needs to come up when he can give it special attention as a word to be spelled, and it needs to come up at fairly regular intervals. The individual spelling list, with a separate spelling period for review of such words, seems the best answer. Then you are sure he studies the words he needs to know.

Some drill is desirable in skills even when the original presentation has been adequate. A student does not often learn to spell a word by writing it once. He must write it several times, perhaps in different contexts, before he retains it permanently. If it takes a class two periods of forty minutes each to learn to do problems in multiplying decimals, it will be profitable to give forty minutes of practice in simply doing such problems later on. Long periods of practice are less beneficial than a little overlearning given soon after the learner first masters the process.

REPEATED REPRODUCTION

We have said that too much overlearning is inefficient. Carried too far, it may be not only inefficient but actually harmful to learning. Too much practice results in satiation and modification.

What happens when we repeat a response too often can be illustrated by a simple experience. Take a sheet of blank paper. Copy the figure on page 164 once, then reproduce it from memory, covering previous attempts each time. Make five figures to the line and spend about five seconds on each one. Make ten lines of five figures each. Then circle the three best and cross out the three poorest drawings.

First of all, analyze your attitude doing such monotonous work. You were probably somewhat interested at first and made some

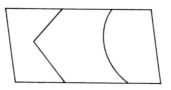

improvement. After a few lines, however, fatigue set in and accuracy suffered. The poorest reproductions were probably near the end, where your attitude became negative. The errors in reproduction were probably modifications in the direction of simplicity and of balance within the structure, making the inner lines symmetrical. In general, as we practice a skill there is a tendency to change what is produced, and too much reproduction results in an active tendency to move away from the model. We say we "tire" of it.

Research in this area includes laboratory work on the reproduction of visual forms and on the modifications a story undergoes as it is repeated. Studies such as these show that:

1. *Repeated reproduction produces continuous modification.* The tendency is not toward fixing what is originally presented or even what is first recalled, but toward reorganization and change.

2. *Modification is in the direction of the familiar, culturally acceptable, simple, and complete.* Each idea is modified to fit in with the learner's existing concept of what it means or should mean, and the greater the degree of difference between the idea and the learner's background the greater the degree of modification. The thought is recast about concepts meaningful to the learner, and even names and idioms are changed from the strange to the familiar. Complex ideas and expressions are simplified. Gaps in content are closed. The structure becomes symmetrical. The meaning is rationalized and incongruities are corrected. Once such a modification is formed, it is relatively stable unless the experience of the learner changes in such a way that the learning must again be recast.

3. *When repetition is forced too far, negativism results.* Satiation distorts normal recall and causes disorganization. The learner refuses to go on; or if he does continue, learning is destroyed.

4. *Individual differences are apparent in this process.* Bright students are more accurate and stable in repeated recall because

they perceive more accurately; slower ones tend to recast the material more. But bright pupils tire of repetition very soon.

. . . IN THE CLASSROOM

Here again we have evidence that learning and recall are geared to the learner's *response,* not to what actually occurs. Even his own response is subject to continuous modification with experience. We have discussed the importance of knowledge of results for the learner. We now know that checking on the accuracy of a reaction is important, not only the first time it is made but continuously during practice, to make sure that what is being practiced remains the correct form. The student may write a corrected spelling the first time or two, but if he is asked to repeat it again and again he may revert to his misspelling or invent a new error.

Illustrations from teaching experience abound. One teacher thought she would correct a child's language by leaving him after school to write fifty lines of "I have gone." He did so, but left a note for the teacher which read "I have went home."

A principal, who was personally signing 250 letters to parents, complained that he simply could not write his name after the seventy-fifth letter; he questioned the spelling, and his hand refused to form his name.

Asking children to carry messages is hazardous. Perhaps the teacher has loaned a favorite pair of scissors to another teacher. She needs them urgently. She asks the child to go to the other teacher, apologize, and ask whether she may use them for a few moments. The child recasts the situation as he sees it, and says "Teacher wants her scissors." Professional relations become strained.

Or perhaps the harassed teacher is unable to make any progress in teaching a child to read. She wonders whether there is ocular imbalance and whether seeing an opthalmologist would help. She asks the child whether he will ask his mother whether it would be convenient for her to come to school and talk over the matter of his reading problem. The child again gives the message as he sees it to his mother, that is, "You've got to come to school tomorrow." The teacher meets a disturbed parent as a result. Messages given to children should be written by the teacher to assure accurate conveyance of the thought.

NEGATIVE PRACTICE

We have seen that too much overlearning or too frequent reproduction is potentially damaging. This fact can be used as a basis for breaking faulty habits. In general, the limited research on negative practice seems to show:

1. *Repetition carried out for long periods may weaken a response.* To achieve this result the response must be practiced with the knowledge that it is wrong, and the practice must be carried beyond the satiation level. Habits of long standing and some nervous habits can be blocked in this way. There is no improvement in the basic problem of which the nervous habit is a symptom, but the specific habit can be blocked by repeating the wrong response many times.

2. *Negative practice is effective in breaking wrong habits, but not in teaching right habits.* This distinction is of particular importance for the teacher in the elementary school. She is concerned chiefly with initial right habits, not with correcting wrong ones.

. . . in the Classroom

Negative practice is useful in working with adults who have deeply fixed faulty habits. Practicing the error on the typewriter, saying each time "This is wrong," and continuing to practice beyond the point where we want to quit, is helpful. It makes us hesitate each time before writing the word to search for the correct form. The same thing may be true for spelling errors. The technique results in bringing interfering habits to conscious thought, and hence in placing them under the control of rational processes.

The chief criticism of negative practice for adults is that it changes habits rather than the imbedded causes of those habits. The individual may stutter as a result of severe emotional conflict. If we teach him to control the stuttering he may develop some other form of symptom.

Negative practice has limited use in the elementary school since the wrong responses with which the teacher is concerned are seldom fixed to the point where it is desirable. Its chief use is in the clinic for adults with persistent and troublesome tics or nervous mannerisms, in combination with general therapy.

Sometimes the teacher does find it useful to use satiation instead of reproof as a method of blocking undesirable behavior. The student who is shooting rubber bands may be provided with a private hallway, target, and generous supply of bands, permitted to shoot to his heart's content, and urged to continue until he refuses to go on. Whether the teacher will use such a procedure will depend upon the relationship with the child in question. Encouraging the student to become fully satiated with an interfering activity and getting him to carry it beyond the point where he wants to do something else may keep him from returning to that activity again.

REMINISCENCE

So far, we have considered only the effect of continuing to practice the skill. We have seen that some overlearning is effective, but that overlearning too long continued is ineffective or even destructive of learning.

Now we turn to a second possibility, that of stopping or interrupting the activity as soon as the child nears mastery. Under those conditions "reminiscence" seems to occur, that is, recall improves after a brief interval of no further learning. The term is used here in a special sense, and not with its popular meaning. It means a tendency for memory to persist without practice.

The common axiom that the best party stops while people still want to stay illustrates this process. It suggests there is a best time for stopping as well as a best one for starting each activity. The teacher is greatly interested in conditions under which such persistence without practice can be attained.

The research on reminiscence is extensive. From these studies the following principles seem to emerge:

1. *Students resist interruption.* They have a strong tendency to complete an activity that has been undertaken. We see the same thing with adults in that jokes that are not completed are often remembered better than those completed. An activity, once undertaken, carries momentum that makes it difficult to block before completion.

2. *Learning which is ended just before mastery results in better immediate retention than learning continued beyond mastery.* If a learner is interrupted when he is about to complete a task, he is likely to remember more of what he has done and to be more likely to resume work when given the opportunity than if he overlearns.

This tendency applies for individuals working together as well as for individuals working alone. Significant amounts of gain occur during the period of rest following learning thus interrupted. Interruption seems to increase the work-energy potential as measured by physiological as well as by psychological methods.

3. *Interruption is most effective near completion of the learning.* This is the point of maximal contact between the subject and the task. The best point for breaking an activity and diverting to another is when the learner is near mastery or has barely achieved it.

4. *The amount gained on interruption increases for a short time, then decreases.* The curve of relationship between the retention increase and the length of rest period is negatively accelerated. In other words, reminiscence is a temporary phenomenon which occurs when learning is stopped at the right place. It affects immediate recall more than it does permanent retention.

5. *These findings hold true only in the absence of emotional tone.* If the interruption is interpreted as failure by the learner, he will repress the experience, avoid the task, and do less well if forced to resume it. In other words, if loss of self-esteem is attached to the interruption, there is no gain. On the other hand, if success is attached to the interruption by the learner, he will think of the task as attractive, boast of his success, and recall still more of what he did. Increasing stress, necessity for maintaining status, or vulnerability to wounds to self-esteem make it impossible to tolerate an inference of failure. If failure is hinted and the learner is sensitive to failure, that fact will destroy any reminiscence.

6. *These findings are most pertinent to learnings in the middle range of difficulty.* Reminiscence is greater with meaningful learning and with that in which interest is high. It is more apparent after a long practice period, when the rate of presentation is fast, and when the material is difficult.

7. *Studies of individual differences show somewhat greater gains in reminiscence for less able learners.* Young children, slow-learning children, and those low in initial achievement gain more from interruption of activity than do more able students.

Reminiscence undoubtedly exists, and the conditions under which it is likely to occur have been described. Why it occurs is less certain. Perhaps mental rehearsal in the rest interval helps, but it does not wholly account for reminiscence. Differential forgetting may be the cause; during rest, the mutual interference of different parts of the learning disappears and retention is facilitated, but again this possibility does not fully account for reminiscence. Neither is it fully explained by the assumption that the learner always anticipates being asked for recall, nor by the fact that each measurement of recall is in itself a practice experience.

One explanation of reminiscence claims that it is the result of incomplete tension systems. An activity, once set in motion, tends to persist through inertia even when the stimulus to activity is removed; that is, there is a tendency toward perseveration. Such unreleased tensions are most effective immediately following the cessation of the activity of which they are a part, so that their effect is greatest on immediate recall.

Whatever the reason, reminiscence occurs as a temporary increase in the amount remembered following a period of rest. It is represented in Figure 7, in schematic form. The dotted line shows what happens when overlearning is used. The solid line shows the rise in immediate recall or "reminiscence effect" produced by stopping at mastery in initial learning. It points to the importance of choosing the right time to stop the learning as well as to start it.

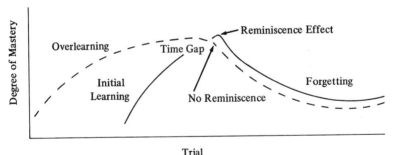

FIGURE 7. PAUSING AT THE POINT OF MASTERY SOMETIMES IMPROVES RETENTION

. . . IN THE CLASSROOM

Implications for teaching are important, but they must be employed with care. We do not interrupt students at will, frustrating them by doing so. However, the teacher's tendency to go right on teaching until learning is perfect is equally bad. An arithmetic process may well be presented just enough to let the learner get a problem right, then temporarily dropped. The play rehearsal may be carried just far enough to get a glimpse of the idea as a whole, then stopped until the following day. A song once sung correctly may well be left for a little while before further practice is attempted. Going on immediately to overlearning seldom pays.

It is often hard for a teacher to stop an activity at just the right place. One teacher asks:

> We had worked through our unit fairly well. The community was all there, the service station and the grocery store doing business, and trucks busy all over the place.
>
> It was time for just a little free play and enjoyment of the unit. The children improvised incidents of all kinds, and when I called time they were quite reluctant to leave. Should I stop them anyway? Should I let them do the same thing tomorrow?

Perhaps the best generalization is that there is a best point for an activity to stop as well as one for it to start. That point can be located by three criteria. The best place for stopping is just at the top of a major gain in learning, when a complete process has been achieved, and before any new material is introduced. The best place for stopping is also the point where everyone is still enjoying the learning, before satiation occurs. Thinking in terms of the curve of learning, the best point for interruption is that at which the curve begins to flatten out at the top of a new gain.

DISTRIBUTION OF PRACTICE

What has already been said brings us to the third way of preventing forgetting, taking advantage of the gains of both reminiscence and overlearning. That is the technique of introducing a learning and carrying it to the point where mastery is in sight, leaving it for a short time, then coming back to it again for rehearsal and review. It is called "distributed" practice, contrasted with "massed" or uninterrupted practice.

The teacher often wonders whether to go on working with a process until it is mastered. If the process is to be broken, at what point should the break occur? What should be done during the rest period when reminiscence is presumably occurring? How often and for how long should she come back for overlearning? A spelling word is mastered one day; the teacher must decide whether to introduce it again, and if so when. The same dilemma occurs in teaching word recognition, arithmetic facts, and other skills.

Investigations of distribution of practice are among the earliest studies of learning. Most experimentation has been done in laboratories. A few attempts have been made to apply the concept to such practical problems as frequency of class meetings, memorizing poetry and prose, learning codes, and learning piano.

The experimental work on distribution of practice shows that:

1. *Distributed practice is uniformly superior to massed practice.* With the amount of time or the number of trials held constant, the efficiency of learning is inversely proportional to the degree of massing and directly proportional to the degree of distribution of practice. The reason for the superiority of distributed practice may be the effect of fatigue in massing, practice in warm-up in distributed practice, differential forgetting during rest in distributed practice, maturation of learning during rest, or more persistent motivation and higher morale in distributed learning. There seems to be a rhythm, alternation, or periodicity of action to which distributed practice conforms and which makes it superior.

2. *Practice periods of decreasing length and rest periods of increasing length represent optimal distribution.* We have already seen that a presentation should be long enough to assure mastery of the concept, and that practicing beyond that point is harmful. Now we find that relatively short practice periods, decreasing in length, are best. Bringing the material to attention repeatedly is more important than holding it in attention for long periods of time.

As for the rest periods, they should be of medium duration, since periods that are too short do not permit reminiscence or forgetting to take place, and those that are too long have no advantage since the greatest forgetting and reminiscence take place just after learning stops. The best point at which to introduce the first rest period corresponds to the point at which reminiscence becomes effective, somewhere between the point at which learning is half complete and where it is just complete.

In any event, the length of practice period and length of rest period must be adjusted to each other. In the most effective schedule, the periods are first long and close together and then become increasingly short and widely spread.

3. *The minimum length of practice period depends upon the nature of the material being learned.* Material that is highly structured and meaningful, and is approached in a logical manner, can profit from more massing than material that is relatively meaningless. Where there are large elements of discovery, as in problem solving, and where variability of attack in the early stages of learning is important, the initial units may also be relatively long. On the other hand, when the learning is routine or drill in nature, long and difficult, presented rapidly, or where the learner is limited in ability, distributed learning is superior to massed learning. In other words, distribution of practice is particularly important for learning that is difficult and tedious.

4. *The advantage of distributed practice is greatest in delayed recall.* We have seen that the reminiscence effect is a temporary phenomenon, affecting immediate rather than delayed recall, and that the effect of overlearning is greatest in permanent retention. Now we see that if we pause for a little while, then present the material again, we have the advantage of both processes.

These principles and the reasons for them are represented diagrammatically in Figure 8. The solid line represents the usual learning and forgetting curves found with continuous practice. The dotted line uses the same total time for learning and for forgetting, but distributes the learning and rest periods in three segments. Let us analyze what happens. In massed or continuous practice we find the usual rapid initial rise, leveling off, and overlearning (*AB*), followed by cessation of the activity. Then there is a rapid initial drop in what is retained, which levels off (*BC*), the height of *C* depending upon degree of overlearning, degree of understanding, and other factors. Here we have assumed the drop will be to one-third permanently retained and that the permanent retention level is reached rather quickly.

Compare the massed practice curve with what happens when there is an equal amount of distributed practice. When learning is interrupted somewhat beyond 50 percent mastery (*D*) there is a brief period of reminiscence because the learning is incomplete, followed by the characteristic forgetting curve. Because the rest interval is short, the forgetting curve does not quite reach its ultimate level. The second learning (*EF*) carries the skill to mastery (*F*), but again limited reminiscence occurs because the

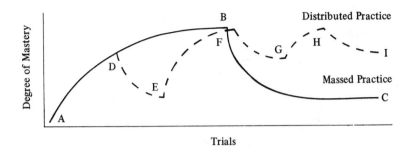

FIGURE 8. DISTRIBUTED PRACTICE USUALLY RESULTS IN GREATER RETENTION
THAN MASSED PRACTICE

learning is barely complete. Forgetting again brings down the skill
sharply (*FG*), but again not as low as before because forgetting is
proportionate to the gain (*EF*). The third learning period (*GH*)
again is followed by a drop, this time to the approximate level of
permanent retention. In the periods of distributed practice, one
learning builds upon the residue of the previous one, reminiscence
occurs, and the final level of retention is significantly above that for
massed practice. The process can be continued until the level of
retention (*I*) is that of mastery (*B, F*).

It is obvious that the rest period must be carefully planned. A
change of activity has the effect of rest, but only if the changed
activity is dissimilar to the learning undertaken. Rest periods from
one learning should be as different in nature as possible from that
learning. We will discuss this matter further when we come to
negative transfer in Chapter 10.

. . . IN THE CLASSROOM

Implications for teaching are many. In planning drills in arithmetic, spelling, and word recognition, it is better to use frequent,
short, spaced periods than to prolong drill at a single time. The
intervals between drills may be filled with work in other subjects, or
with review of easy and quite different skills. Learning a list of new
spelling words may be followed by a day of free writing, introducing an arithmetic process by a day of work on written problems, and
intensive work on words by listening to a story read by the teacher.

An illustration from the teaching of arithmetic may clarify the meaning. A fourth-grade teacher observed the following schedule in introducing long division:

Monday: Introduced the process by developing need from a plan we were drawing, reviewing short division, demonstrating the process several times.

Tuesday: Demonstrated the process again, had students tell me what to do at each step, then gave them problems to do individually. Let those who had difficulty work at the board where I could watch.

Wednesday: Gave them a few long-division problems to do at their seats, and corrected papers with them.

Thursday: Gave them some problems in multiplication and subtraction for review.

Friday: Gave them some long-division problems again. Applied the process to our plans.

Monday: Gave them some long-division problems. Used the rest of the period applying the process to help them with using the subdivisions on a ruler.

Tuesday through Thursday: Used these days for review and for practice in use of ruler.

Friday: Reviewed long division again.

Similarly, applying the concept of distribution of practice to the teaching of spelling, one supervisor, who combines individual and class approaches, suggests:

Monday: Individual study of individual lists of words.

Tuesday: Partner study of same lists.

Wednesday: Partner testing and checking of individual lists.

Thursday: Individual study of words still missed.

Friday: Class test on twenty words studied by class for the week, and class pretest on twenty new words for week following. Words missed recorded in individual books.

An illustration of distribution of practice within a shorter period of time is cited by a student observer.

The reading period in the second grade is varied in such a way that the child will learn and also have fun. One group will read first; after reading, they will relax by working with paints, drawing or painting anything they wish. Then the children return to their desks and resume the assignment given at the end of the reading period. The rest or painting period is equal in length to the reading period.

In memorizing materials and in study for examinations, the most effective procedure for permanent learning is to distribute the practice periods. The student should go over his notes once, come back another day for review, and so on until the time for the examination arrives. Cramming, or massed learning, will be nearly as effective for the examination, but the material will be quickly forgotten afterward. Frequent tests which force distribution of learning are effective for this reason, as well as for the greater degree of activity they require.

Administrative problems such as class scheduling are somewhat more complex. For permanence of learning, class meetings that are one hour in length for twelve weeks have some advantage over class meetings two hours in length for six weeks. When five meetings a week are compared with four or three, the results are clouded. In most cases, however, research has measured only retention at the end of the course, and not retention after longer periods when the full advantage of distribution of practice would become apparent.

In areas where the material is highly meaningful and in problem solving, however, there is little difference between massed and distributed learning. Films may apparently be used in massed form, because of the many intensity factors which keep learning at a relatively high level. The advantages of distributed practice are greatest for learning that a particular learner finds relatively difficult or routine.

SUMMER LOSS

One of the most practical problems of forgetting in school is loss during the summer vacation. Let us see whether we can in any way predict what will happen during long periods of rest from school activities, and what ways of preventing or counteracting forgetting are effective.

Research has been concerned chiefly with the extent of loss during summer vacation for various subjects and various age levels. There has been some comparison of summer and winter losses and gains, some study of the effect of summer-school attendance, and some study of the effectiveness of fall review in restoring the achievement level to that of the previous spring.

In general, the studies of loss during summer vacation seem to show:

1. *The more specific the skill the greater the loss.* Spelling and arithmetic fundamentals uniformly show large losses, while content fields such as literature, geography and science are relatively stable. This is in agreement with what we said about essential level of recall.

2. *The less complete the mastery of the skill, the greater the loss.* Children who are just beginning to read lose their skill, while upper-grade students show gains. The loss in arithmetic fundamentals is greater in middle grades than after the processes are more firmly fixed in the seventh and eighth grades. There is little loss in arithmetic reasoning at any point since it is more closely related to intelligence and reading comprehension than to arithmetic fundamentals as such. The student will be able to use independently during vacations only those skills that he has mastered.

3. *The less the transfer to out-of-school life, the greater the loss.* Upper-grade students go to libraries and summer camp and therefore gain in reading and nature study. They do not do arithmetic problems, nor use correct language at play, nor write lists of spelling words except in the classroom; these skills show loss. In a sense, vacation is a test of the transfer value of a given curriculum. If there is a consistent loss over a wide grade range, it may well be that something is wrong with that curriculum for the children pursuing it.

4. *Individual variability in loss during vacations is great.* Bright students tend to gain more and lose less than average pupils, perhaps because of their greater independence of action and degree of mastery. More important, what the learner loses depends on his activities during the summer. If his is a home that encourages library reading and summer camp he will show gains in reading and natural science. If there is no provision for special activities, he may lose in those fields. The differences in degree of loss for various content fields are affected by the pattern of life in the home from which the student comes. Many teachers help pupils plan activities for the summer which supplement the work of the school in valuable ways.

5. *Loss during the summer vacation can be slowed by spring review.* Intensive spring review of from two weeks to a month in arithmetic fundamentals and spelling serves as a buffer against subsequent summer loss. This is an illustration of wise use of overlearning.

6. *Summer-school attendance results in little or no gain in achievement, but it does prevent the deterioration of skills.* It is questionable, however, whether the loss of supplementary activities such as summer camp, playground, reading, and family group activities may not more than counterbalance the gains of summer school. Further, some studies show that summer drill in skills may be followed in the fall by lower achievement than that which follows normal summer activities. If the overlearning during summer is too prolonged it takes on the characteristics of negative practice suggested above.

7. *Fall review is effective as a way of regaining what has been lost during the summer.* Two to six weeks of review will bring students back to the point they had reached before the summer vacation. Fall review has been criticized as unnecessary; but the review has distinct value if it is interpreted, not as reteaching the past year's work, but as recalling the familiar elements necessary for proceeding with the next year's activities. In other words, the review should occur in new contexts and serve as a base for the next steps. Review is most necessary in skills such as spelling and arithmetic fundamentals.

. . . IN THE CLASSROOM

It is clear, then, that the teacher must expect a pattern of differential forgetting over long vacations. If the student knows a skill well, can use it independently, and finds it useful in out-of-school activities, the vacation will cause little loss and may result in gain. If he is just beginning to learn a skill, if he cannot use it independently, and if his out-of-school activities do not allow it to function, that skill will show a rapid loss during the vacation. Arithmetic fundamentals and spelling are particularly susceptible to loss under such conditions. That loss, however, can be retarded by a little spring review, by summer-school attendance, or best of all by fall review in a context. Some combination of all these techniques for minimizing summer loss is probably the best plan.

The findings also suggest that the teacher may well be cautious in judging a student's achievement after a long vacation. Achievement tests given in September may be misleading. Judgments about how well a class was taught last year on the basis of the first few weeks' experience with it are similarly hazardous. Only after there has been opportunity for relearning can judgments be made. A sixth-grade teacher says:

> I spend the last three weeks in the spring going over the spelling lists for the semester, giving review drills for the various arithmetic processes, letting students reread their own and others' compositions, and tying together the loose ends of the unit. We try to relearn anything that may have been forgotten.
>
> One thing I do, too, is to spend some time in talking about plans for the summer vacation. I am careful that the students all make several trips to the public library, have time to browse, and have library cards. I see that representatives of youth groups, playgrounds, and summer camps come in to talk of what they are offering. We talk about writing letters, and of what we can do on our own with free time. Often summer reading helps a student a great deal, or a trip to summer camp introduces him to science.
>
> Then, in the fall, I give them a chance to talk about what they have done during the summer. I also approach new processes in arithmetic by reviewing what I had taught last year, and am not concerned if I have to teach some of the same spelling words over again. In the fall, such review is essential.

IMPLICATIONS

From all of these areas of research, the following implications for teaching emerge:

1. Expect some forgetting after every learning. Expect rapid forgetting immediately after learning. Expect rapid forgetting of new or formal learnings.

2. Adapt procedures for preventing forgetting to the kind of use you expect the learner to have for the material. Teach skills to the level of permanent recall. Teach most content to the level of recognition. Do not bring attitudes and appreciations to the level of recognition.

3. Provide overlearning to get permanent retention at the level of recall. Limit overlearning to 50 percent of the time needed for mastery. Check the accuracy of practice to prevent modification. Stop overlearning at any sign of satiation or negativism. Use negative practice to block persistent faulty habits.

4. Stop a learning activity near the point of mastery. Break it as near that point as possible. Avoid any implication of failure in the interruption.

5. Distribute the learning periods to get permanent retention at

the level of recall. Make the initial period long enough to review the whole process or material. Decrease the length of practice period systematically. Adapt the length of rest period to the length of work period. Use different and easy activities during the rest period.

6. Plan to counteract loss in formal skills during the summer vacation. Give special attention to skills that are new and formal. Review for a few weeks in the spring. Help plan summer activities which use skills and supplement content. Review in the fall as a basis for the next year's work.

EXERCISES IN APPLICATION

1. Mrs. Small will have a fourth-grade class in September. She can expect patterns of differential forgetting over the summer vacation. In what subject should she expect greatest loss? Do the areas of greatest loss show anything about the value of the curriculum of the preceding year? What will be the nature of the difference for children attending summer school? Is review in June or in September the more advantageous? Why?

2. You have budgeted your time to study for finals so that you have eight hours to spend on each test, and are making a time schedule for the week. Your test in educational psychology comes last. When shall you begin to study for it? What time schedule would you propose? Why?

3. You have been studying intensively for an examination, and are having difficulty in concentrating. You decide you need to rest. What kind of rest will best serve to improve your ability to study and your retention of the material? What kind of activity? How long? Taken at what point in learning? Why?

4. Would you use negative practice with a first-grade child who continued to call "where" "there"? With a sixth-grade child who constantly spelled "said" "sed"? Why? What is the difference between the two situations?

5. A child is asked to repeat a somewhat long lesson assignment to several of his classmates each of whom is confined to his home. Will he repeat it accurately? If not, what kinds of modification will he probably make? Why?

6. A third-grade child is practicing spelling words. Should his teacher ask him to write each word once, three times, or ten times? To what learning principle is this decision related?

7. For which of the following types of learning situation is systematic review highly important: scientific principles, spelling, language usage, literature, arithmetic facts, word recognition, arithmetic problem solving, foreign language? Can you describe the type of learning situation in which

review is important and distinguish it from that in which it is less important? Why?

8. Miss Dingman teaches spelling through simply supplying to the children the words requested in creative writing, relying on normal word repetition to fix the correct spelling of essential words. Mr. Ellender, on the other hand, has each child keep a list of the words he requests in creative writing, and uses that list as a basis for individual review and testing each week. Which procedure would you advocate? Why? On the basis of what learning principle?

9. Which reading group will require relatively more word drill in a first grade—the one that is advanced in reading or the one that is having difficulty in learning its first words? Why? Can you generalize the same principle to the giving of assignments for homework in high-school algebra?

10. Two teachers of third grade were discussing whether word drill in reading was really necessary. Teacher A pointed out that reading textbooks are so constructed that they provide normal word repetition, and drill is not needed. Teacher B stressed the need for emphasizing free reading, with no systematic review. Which teacher is right? State psychological principles supporting your point of view.

SUGGESTIONS FOR FURTHER READING

Babrick, H. P. "The Ebb of Retention." *Psych. Rev., 70,* 60–73, 1965. A critical analysis of conventional retention curves and a suggested modification.

Bilodeau, E. A., and Ina McD. Bilodeau. "Motor-skills Learning." *Ann. Rev. Psych., 12,* 243–280, 1961. A somewhat technical review of psychological research, 1945–1959, on motor-skill learning, including feedback, transfer, and practice among other variables.

Briggs, L. J., and Nancy L. Hamilton. "Meaningful Learning and Retention: Practice and Feedback Variables." *Rev. Educ. Res., 34,* 545–558, 1964. A review of learning of paired associates, isolated facts, concepts, problem solving, and social behavior with special reference to feedback, reward, distribution of practice, and transfer.

Kausler, D. H., ed. *Readings in Verbal Learning.* New York: Wiley, 1966. A broad selection of papers published since 1952 on verbal learning, including sections on transfer and retention.

Keppel, G. "Verbal Learning and Memory." *Ann. Rev. Psych., 19,* 169–202, 1968. A somewhat technical review of learning studies, touching on transfer, retention, and other factors.

Levy, C. M., and Karen Hartnagle. "The Psychology of Memory—1965: a Bibliography." *Perceptual and Motor Skills, 25,* 573–582, 1967. A listing of 255 contributions to the psychology of memory and forgetting published in 1965.

Miller, N. E. "Laws of Learning Relevant to Biological Bases." *Proceedings of the Amer. Philos. Soc., 111*, 315–325, 1967. A discussion of short-term and long-term memory in relation to interference and close temporal association from the standpoint of research.

Peterson, L. R. "Short-term Verbal Memory and Learning." *Psych. Rev., 73*, 193–207, 1966. An analysis of short-term memory storage within a long-term learning mechanism.

Underwood, B. J. "Ten Years of Massed Practice on Distributed Practice." *Psych. Rev., 68*, 229–247, 1961. A summary of research on distributed practice in verbal learning, with concepts suggested to explain the findings.

Ward, L. B. "Reminiscence and Rote Learning." *Psych. Monog., 49*, #4, 1937. A classic study of reminiscence over short intervals of time.

Transferring Learning

So far we have been concerned with learning new material and making that learning permanent. But the teacher often wonders whether the child who uses good language in the classroom is similarly careful on the playground, whether the girl who has perfect spelling papers spells correctly when she writes letters at home, whether the class that knows its arithmetic processes will show to advantage with the next teacher, and whether any of the things she has so carefully taught will remain with the child ten or twenty years hence. The teacher is not content to teach specific skills, no matter how well or how permanently. She must also teach so that learning will function in new and different situations, and in the remote future.

In discussing transfer we are dealing with one of the most complex and far-reaching problems in learning. Mental functions are interdependent and interrelated. Every experience changes the capacity for new experience. Transfer occurs whenever a previous learning influences the acquisition of a second learning. For this reason, transfer is inherently dependent upon the effectiveness of the original learning. We have learned that structure and meaning and the formation of concepts are the keys to effective learning and retention. We have found that transfer is interwoven with degree of guidance and with problem solving.

Transfer effects may, however, be either positive or negative. We say the transfer is positive if previous experience aids learning a new task. The new learning is sensed as being similar to an earlier experience, and the earlier learning serves a mediating function in establishing a relation between the new experience and a similar kind of behavior.

We say that transfer is negative if experience inhibits the learning or performance of either task. Then the new learning is sensed as being similar to another experience, but the behavior learned for the old experience must be changed in the new situation and finer discriminations learned. If the originally learned response is adequate in the new situation, the transfer will be positive; if the originally learned response is inadequate in the new situation, the transfer will be negative. We will analyze the conditions under which negative transfer occurs at a later point, and attempt to show the unitary nature of the whole transfer phenomenon.

FORMAL DISCIPLINE

Early in the twentieth century a controversy arose between the champions of so-called "faculty" psychology and those of the newer experimental forms. The earlier theoretical group had contended that training of any kind was actually training of the mind as a whole, and that specific practice on a skill had a general effect on the whole behavior of the individual. The argument gained increased significance since it coincided with the introduction of high-school education for all, with its query of whether the traditional college-preparatory curriculum which stressed Latin and formal mathematics was suitable for all. Proponents of the doctrine of formal discipline took the position that the generalized effects of the traditional subjects made them appropriate learnings for all students, while the experimental psychologists and the functionalists in education insisted that more practical learnings should be substituted.

Early experimentation and critical discussion showed that transfer from the conventional subjects to general activities is far less than has been claimed. The doctrine of formal discipline became a straw man toward which were directed many of the attacks of the educational reformers. It soon became apparent, however, that although the doctrine of formal discipline in its extreme statement is inaccurate, to say that learning is entirely specific is likewise inaccurate. Research was then directed toward defining the conditions under which positive transfer occurs, and the extent of its influence on learning.

Summarizing the early studies directed toward the doctrine of formal discipline, we find that:

1. *Transfer does exist.* There are very few situations that are entirely new; hence old learnings always affect what we learn from the new. Specific skills, methods of attack, and attitudes carry over to subsequent learning. To deny the existence of transfer is to deny the evidence.

2. *Transfer is much more limited than is generally realized.* The doctrine of formal discipline assumed a generality of transfer that does not exist. Training in logical analysis helps in analyzing logical material. Training in solving problems in arithmetic helps in solving problems in arithmetic. Training in understanding fables helps in understanding new fables. Reaching decisions with regard to situations helps in reaching decisions in new situations. Intercorrelations between different types of learning situations are very low, however. No amount of training increases greatly the individual's ability to reason in general. The gains are specific, and transferable only when the same method of attack facilitates the handling of similar material. Instead of thinking in terms of "training the mind" we now think of positive and negative transfer to highly similar situations or of stimulus generalization and response generalization.

. . . in the Classroom

A college student reported:

I remember very clearly the first day of the geometry class. We were told that it was the purpose of mathematics to develop our minds, just as physical education developed our bodies. In physical education we lifted weights, swung Indian clubs, and did push-ups to develop muscles in our arms, so that we would be strong. In mathematics we were to learn theorems and formulas, which we might well not understand or be able to apply, but which would develop something comparable to a "mental muscle" that could then be used to solve any kind of problem that might come along.

A junior-high-school counselor much later found the assumption of the existence of formal discipline in another context.

I was trying to explain to a class of bright eighth-grade students the college-entrance requirement of a foreign language. They were able to understand the practical value of Spanish in Southern California, and perhaps other modern languages for travel. I tried to explain that English was derived from other languages and study of other languages would help in English. They countered with the argument why not study Saxon if English is partly derived from Saxon, or why not just study English origins instead of a foreign language? I pointed out that Latin was still used in law and in medicine. One boy quoted his father, a lawyer, as saying legal meanings of Latin phrases were so specialized that a previous knowledge of Latin was a hindrance instead of a help. In desperation, I pointed out that formal learning of the kind used in studying a language was a good test of ability to do such formal learning in college. They pointed out that standardized tests could do the same thing with much less loss of time. Finally we settled for the fact that it was good to know about how other people lived and that a foreign language was a key to another culture; and that anyway there was no logical way of explaining some educational requirements!

Another time I was talking with the mother of a girl who was failing in the first semester of Latin for the second time. I urged letting the girl drop the course, take no language for a year, then take up an entirely new one such as Spanish in order to have a fresh start. The mother was not so much concerned with the girl's missing Latin as with the effect of dropping a subject. She asked whether it would not thereby cause the girl to back away in the face of any difficulty, to become a moral weakling. I'm not sure I was successful in explaining that all of us find *some* things difficult, and that this one situation would transfer less widely than the mother supposed.

The findings on formal discipline mean that the school cannot claim to be preparing students for all types of situations through remotely related activities. It means that the situations the individual meets in the classroom must be highly similar to those which he will encounter in out-of-school life if any transfer is to be expected. It means that classroom situations must be lifelike, and that the classroom must constantly interact with life situations through discussion, observation, and participation. The school cannot be a place where learning is contained within four walls. It must be a segment of life, constantly interacting with other segments, if what is learned in school is to become effective in life.

POSITIVE TRANSFER

The fundamental nature of positive transfer is clear when we analyze the implications for teaching. If the student learns only the specific skills he is taught in school, and can at most use no more than those identical skills as they occur in life situations, the concept of the function of the school must be changed radically.

Instead, we assume that we are teaching skills, attitudes, methods of work, and information which the student will transfer broadly to adult life, that we are molding the adult behavior not only in specifics but in many more significant ways. Caught between the fallacy of the doctrine of formal discipline and the fact that schools are charged with preparation for a broad range of life activities, we must find out just how transfer occurs and how we can secure the maximum amount.

The experimental literature on positive transfer includes both laboratory studies of stimulus and response generalization and studies of transfer in foreign languages, spelling, arithmetic, and scientific thinking.

Such studies show that:

1. *Positive transfer occurs whenever a specific response already learned is to be made in a similar new situation.* This is the theory of identical elements. There may be partial identity of content, or the use of a common method. A spelling word learned in writing a story is likely to be spelled correctly in a letter. A word learned in the reading of one page is usually recognized in a different context. A word element which is constant for a group of words may be pointed out and new words worked out more easily as a result. Training in memorizing poetry will help the learner to memorize new poems.

2. *Positive transfer occurs whenever a generalization already learned applies in a new situation.* An attitude toward arithmetic formed in the third grade may affect a woman's ability to balance her checkbook. Experience in logical reasoning gained in geometry may under favorable conditions carry over later to estimating heights. A study procedure learned in history may carry over to economics. General principles, modes of attack, and sets to perform are the most common transfer agents. The process of learning is one of taking specifics and gradually developing concepts from them, as we have seen in our study of problem solving. The process of transfer reverses the process, taking concepts previously learned and applying them to new situations. Both learning and transfer are essentially dynamic processes in which the individual reconstructs

and modifies his behavior and creates new patterns of action on the basis of the old.

3. *Positive transfer is more likely to occur when there is conscious teaching for transfer.* Transfer is not automatic. For transfer, the material must be taught not as a specific, but for broader use. Wide experience and factual knowledge do not assure transfer. Transfer is the result of conscious effort, of conscious generalization and application while learning.

Transfer is favored by a learning set directed toward classification, generalization, relationships, and position within a logical learning structure. It is much less likely to occur when generalization is undirected, and when the relationship to other learnings is a mechanical one.

The teacher may aid transfer by suggesting that certain experiences may be useful, proposing a method of study, providing knowledge of related fields, encouraging the development of skill in manipulating ideas, stimulating systematic questioning of the evidence, teaching the ability to apply statistical analysis and inference, and making the individual aware of methods he is using and might use. The ability to organize materials and methods to promote the maximum degree of positive transfer is the mark of a superior teacher. The learner will transfer to some extent on his own initiative when two situations are highly similar, but conscious teaching for transfer will make it possible for the individual to apply his learning more widely through analysis of similarities between the old and the new. Ability to transfer is an important factor in perception, insight, reasoning and originality.

4. *The more effective the original teaching, the greater the degree of transfer.* Transfer is more likely to occur when the original learning is complete and accurate, when the materials are meaningful and structured, when the transfer situation is highly similar to the learning situation, when the material provides for continuous reconstruction of experience, when the attitudes toward learning both the original and the transferred materials are favorable, and when the time between original learning and transfer is relatively short.

5. *Individual differences are apparent in the ability to transfer.* Bright students and older ones generalize easily; hence they are able to transfer their learnings more widely. In general, how much trans-

fer occurs for a given individual depends on the material to be learned, his experience, his desire to learn, and his training in generalization and transfer procedures.

. . . in the Classroom

Transfer is a conscious process. Facts should be organized to stress relationships and concepts rather than being taught as isolated skills or bits of knowledge. The field of instruction and the field of transfer must be closely related. There is no clear demonstration of transfer in any broad sense. For transfer to occur, school situations must be specific, and specifically related to functional and comparable life situations.

These findings imply that, in teaching arithmetic and mathematics, the teacher will provide for concept formation and functional application in addition to teaching manipulation of the symbols which represent them, constantly showing the interrelationships between experience and the symbols. New concepts will be presented in familiar context, and experience will be provided in many different situations to assure transfer. The teacher will not assume that, once having learned subtraction or multiplication, the learner can use them in any situation. Instead, she will reteach him subtraction, multiplication, and long division in each new context he meets. The geometry teacher who wishes to improve ability in logical reasoning will not teach geometry alone, but will help the student to analyze the thought processes he is using and to apply the same kind of analysis to a wide range of nonmathematical problems.

Similarly, in content fields such as the sciences the teacher will emphasize experience in finding generalizations and study techniques. Students will be taught to look for scientific method and for practical applications of a science, and to apply their knowledge to the interpretation of popular scientific literature. They will have lessons in outlining which stress thought-getting and thought-giving processes. A method of approach to subject matter, once learned, transfers to other context fields in which the same mode of attack is applicable.

The teacher will stress the development of logical reasoning in all content fields, and use problem solving as a method of approach to give experience in logical reasoning. She will teach students to identify relevant facts, select and organize them, make inferences, distinguish fact from opinion, and recognize situations in which conclusions cannot be drawn because of insufficient evidence. With such training the students will improve significantly, not only in the content presented, but in reasoning in similar situations as well. Such learning is relatively permanent.

When we come to language learning, including the learning of spelling, the findings are mixed. Studies suggest that the influence of studying Latin helps somewhat with English grammar and vocabulary and with spelling English words of Latin origin. The study of Latin seems to interfere, however, with the spelling of English words not derived from Latin and with good oral and written expression in English, and to develop overanalytical reading habits that seem to transfer to English. Transfer effects from the study of a foreign language to the study of English are small.

Studies of the teaching of spelling rules and principles show similarly mixed results. There is little positive transfer in languages and spelling because languages, and especially English, are not logically organized bodies of knowledge. A language consists of many specific and often unique learnings. Because of the nonlogical nature of most languages there can be little generalization and therefore little positive transfer. There are, on the contrary, distinct hazards of negative transfer.

NEGATIVE TRANSFER

We have said that transfer may be either positive or negative, that positive transfer occurs if the originally learned response is adequate in a new situation, but that if the originally learned response is not adequate and new discriminations must be learned, transfer will be negative. Now let us see what kinds of school situations cause negative transfer.

The teacher sometimes finds that going on to a new learning actually seems to destroy what she has taught previously. Sometimes she thinks the child can recognize "was." She introduces "saw" and finds that the child cannot recognize either "was" or "saw" but uses them indiscriminately. Or the child may be having trouble in selecting the correct spelling of "to," "two," and "too" for a given context. She explains the meaning of all three forms, then finds he uses any one in any context. Or she may give "friend" and "receive" in the same spelling list, explain the spelling rule and its exceptions, then find the child more confused than ever. In all of these cases transfer is occurring, but the result is confusion instead of facilitation in the new learning.

Stimulus generalization and response generalization apply to negative as well as to positive transfer. No stimulus or response is ever limited to one specific cue or act. Associative inhibition, proactive inhibition, and retroactive inhibition refer to special kinds of negative transfer. We will not attempt to detail the differences between them here, but rather to determine what the conditions are which create interference between two learnings, no matter what the sequence may be. The teacher is usually concerned with two learnings, both of which are essential. She wishes to present each so that there will be a minimum of interference from the other.

From the many studies of various aspects of negative transfer, the following principles emerge:

1. *Transfer is sometimes negative, one learning actively interfering with another.* Once a habit has been developed in a given situation, learning a new response is more difficult than it would be had the previous habit not been established. If the two responses must be differentiated and given appropriately to the same stimulus, they become confused or compete for survival. Negative transfer is most pronounced when the new learning is first introduced, declining as the new learning becomes more firmly fixed as an independent concept.

The theoretical implications for forgetting are important. It is the findings on negative transfer that have led to the abandonment of the concept that forgetting is caused by disuse. Instead, we now think of forgetting as caused by active interference from new learnings.

2. *Negative transfer is decreased when rest immediately follows learning.* The period between learning and recall should be a relatively inactive one. A normal amount of sleep favors retention more than a normal amount of conscious activity, and there is proportional advantage for rest for shorter periods as well. The effect of rest and sleep on retention of nonessential and meaningless material is greater than on meaningful material. In other words, meaning is an important factor in preventing negative transfer.

3. *The greater the degree of similarity between two learnings, the greater the amount of negative transfer.* When a new response must

be made to an identical stimulus, as in the case of a new spelling for a word pronounced in the same way as an old one, there is confusion. When there has been teaching for generalization between tasks and a new task is introduced which must be differentiated from the old, transfer is negative, that is, the learner generalizes but fails to differentiate. If the stress is on relationships between the two responses, confusion will result. If, on the other hand, the student's previous experience or the teacher's stress on meaning is unique to the new response, the stress on meaning will retard negative transfer. In other words, both negative and positive transfer occur when two situations are similar; but if there are essential differences which must be noted, we call the transfer negative because it interferes with exact reproduction of the new response alone. Anything that destroys the structure or isolation of each individual learning may create negative transfer.

4. *The greater the degree of similarity in external conditions between two learnings, the greater the amount of negative transfer.* When two similar learnings that must be differentiated are taught immediately following each other, or when recall for an earlier learning is asked for immediately after a new learning, negative transfer is increased. Separating the two learnings as completely as possible in time will reduce negative transfer. Similar learnings that occur in the same place are more likely to be confused than those that occur in different places. Similar learnings that come through the same sensory mode are more likely to be confused than those that come through different sensory modes. This finding holds for learnings coming through the left as opposed to the right hand. Learnings of similar affective value are more likely to be confused than those of different emotional tone. When two similar learnings occur under the same learning set or by the same learning method, they are more likely to be confused than if they occur under different learning sets or by different methods. Whatever contributes to bringing together the two learnings that must be distinguished increases the amount of negative transfer.

5. *Learning that is complete is less susceptible to negative transfer than learning that is incomplete.* Overlearning, or learning beyond the point where the student has mastered the material, will help to prevent later interference from new learnings. Stressing the new learning when an old learning is incomplete fixes the new learning but destroys the old. When a learning is long or difficult,

more time must be given it before the new learning is introduced. In other words, if two learnings are to be differentiated, it is important to learn one completely before going on to the second.

6. *Negative transfer creates disturbed behavior.* The effect of confusion is erratic behavior. It is similar to that described as the effect of failure, of blocking in the solution of a problem. The fact that confusion creates such disturbed behavior is a strong argument for preventing negative transfer in learning.

7. *Studies of individual differences show few consistent trends.* There is some suggestion that negative transfer decreases with age, since experience and wealth of association help to prevent negative transfer. The brighter student transfers more learnings than the slow-learning one, and differentiates more easily. The result is that the bright pupil makes errors in transfer where materials are not logical, as in nonphonetic spelling, but avoids them where previous generalizations apply to new situations. In other words, the rapid learner tends to transfer through concepts. If the learning is consistent he shows more positive transfer, but if the learning is inconsistent, he shows more negative transfer.

. . . IN THE CLASSROOM

Inferences from such studies are particularly pertinent to the teaching of language. Experiences in learning two new languages at the same time are of interest. A college instructor reported:

I should have known better. Because I had taken so much Latin in high school, I was relieved of all language requirements in college, and again for my master's degree. Then there came the Ph.D., and I needed a reading knowledge of both French and German.

I wanted to get both language examinations out of the way the next year, so I systematically set about learning them. I took French at the local high school on Monday and Wednesday nights, and German on Tuesday and Thursday nights, and reviewed for both over the week end.

The net result was that I could read either language fairly well. French was easier than German, because of my Latin background. But when it came to composition I was lost. I spoke or wrote a mixture of French and German that was comprehensible to no one but myself.

Even an experienced linguist had difficulty:

I already knew French and Italian and German. I was offered a position with a firm in South America if I could learn Spanish and Portuguese. I must be ready the next summer, but it seemed easy.

Instead of taking one language each semester, I took both during the fall. I found myself trying to figure out just which form was Portuguese and which Spanish, and substituting Italian and occasionally French. Keep your languages separate if you want them to be useful.

Parents often ask whether a parental language which is not English should be taught to the child in infancy. Such teaching usually makes it more difficult for him to learn English than if English were his first and basic language. It may even cause inhibition, confusion, and delayed reading. Similarly, if the student is taught to write a second language before his writing habits in English are fixed, he is confused. A child who transferred from an English- to a Spanish-speaking school in the third grade applied Spanish vowel sounds to the spelling of English words, to the constant confusion of her English-speaking correspondents.

There are applications also to the teaching of word recognition in reading. Children often confuse "was" and "saw," "when" and "then," "think" and "thank." Teachers sometimes present the two words together, compare them, and hope the child can keep them apart in that way. The result is still greater confusion. Instead, the teacher should choose one of the pair, make it as vivid as possible, present it often, and make the child responsible for recognizing it until he has no trouble. Then she should introduce the second word and teach it independently in a similar fashion. Any comparison between the two before each is independently fixed will increase the confusion.

Similar questions arise in the teaching of spelling and language rules, and here the research is extensive. The English language is not a rational language, and English spelling is particularly irrational. Since spelling is irrational, there is little to gain through rationalizing the probable letter to associate with a given sound. The student who described a train on which he was riding as "airkundishund" was being quite logical. It is helpful to have the student pronounce the word to see that he has a correct auditory impression, but to go beyond that may be more harmful than helpful. Attention called to how a sound is written in a given word may result in transfer which will produce misspelling in another word.

Such hope as exists in applying generalization to learning spelling is to be found in teaching methods of adding suffixes and prefixes to base words to make derived forms. Even though a few rules are widely applicable and relatively free from exceptions, they are difficult to teach and still more difficult to apply under the stress of spelling and composition. When they are taught, they should be developed inductively through presenting a number of words to which the rule applies, letting the learner form his own generalization, and helping him to apply it in new situations.

The rule for "ie" and "ei" is not among those recommended. The problem is illustrated in an experience of a student observer:

It was that same spelling lesson that was taught so well. The children were writing thank-you notes to a speaker who had brought in branding irons for their western unit. There were five words, including "friend" and "receive." The presentation was admirable, except for these two words.

First the teacher presented "friend," asked how it was used in the letter, and had the children write it. Then she presented "receive" and did the same thing. But she added, "You see, the *ei* is just the opposite of what it is in 'friend.' The rule that will help you to keep them straight is [and she gave it]. Besides, do you notice that 'friend' ends in 'end?' " When the test was given, everyone had all the words right except "friend" and "receive," and I think I know why more of them got "friend" right than "receive."

A third-grade teacher illustrates this kind of confusion in the case of "to," "two" and "too."

The children were always getting them mixed up. In desperation I put each word on the board in turn, explained how it was used, and had children give illustrations. They seemed to understand, but still they used the wrong spellings. They remembered there were three ways, and what they were, but couldn't remember which to use in any one place.

I talked the matter over in the lunch room with one of the first-grade teachers, and she told me how she straightens out confusions in reading. So I decided to try a different plan with the next class. I taught them "two" first, because it was the most colorful and meaningful of the group. They had it in language and in arithmetic and in spelling, until everyone knew that word. Then I taught them "to," which they were using anyway much of the time. Finally, after a week or so, we came to "too," which I taught simply as a language drill, testing by whether "also" could be substituted. They seemed to get the idea. Only then did we say anything about the fact that the sound could be written in three different ways, and bring them together for comparison.

POSITIVE AND NEGATIVE TRANSFER AS A SINGLE PROCESS

We have examined the conditions under which positive and negative transfer occur. There is a striking degree of resemblance between the two. The question then becomes one of how to tell what will happen in a particular learning situation.

The teacher must decide whether that which she is about to teach may be forgotten as a specific and the concept merged with others. If the specific may be safely forgotten, if she is teaching primarily for the sake of a broader principle, the new learning may be presented with the old and comparisons made. If, on the other hand, it must be remembered in just the form in which she is teaching it, as the spelling of a word or a foreign phrase, she will exert every effort to isolate it from other similar learnings. She will present the two words that might be confused in different contexts, at different times, by different methods, and without comparison.

Theoretical discussions suggest principles which apply to the whole field of transfer, whether positive or negative. It seems that:

1. *All learnings tend to merge.* Any experience moves toward assimilation with all past experiences and reaches forward and affects future experiences as well. Each individual's experience becomes unitary. Positive and negative transfer are not two different mental processes. It is a single two-way reinforcement and interference phenomenon. In school the problem is especially complex because we are interested not in saving just one learning but in developing both.

2. *If two learnings can merge without damage to the usefulness of the learning, transfer is said to be positive.* A child learns to reason about an arithmetic problem. He is taught to apply the same process to a problem of classroom behavior. He remembers the process of analysis and forgets what the arithmetic problem was. The teacher's objective is achieved. A student learns that a given psychological principle was demonstrated in a particular experiment. He applies the principle to designing a new experiment or to teaching. He forgets about the particular experiment, but little is lost because it is the concept that is important. In both cases we say the merging of learnings results in positive transfer.

3. *If merging the two learnings destroys the usefulness of the learning, transfer is said to be negative.* In other words, the difference between negative and positive transfer lies, not in the process, but in the *end result of learning desired by the teacher.* A child learns to spell "friend" in the context of the *ie* rule. He is immediately asked to learn "receive," an exception to the rule. He remembers they both had *i* and *e* and were covered by a rule given him,

but does not remember the details of either the words or the rule. He is confused and interchanges the spelling of the two words. Here each learning must be retained in its unique form. Stressing the rule, or introducing the generalizing process, results in negative transfer. In other words, when there must be discrimination between two incompatible responses in recall, the transfer will be negative.

4. *Essentially the same conditions contribute to positive and to negative transfer.* Any learning condition that brings the two learnings together increases the amount of transfer. Similarity of meaning or of learning conditions, generalization between the learning situations, teaching by similar methods, and teaching together in time all promote transfer. Giving the learnings different contexts, separating them in time, teaching them by different methods, and completing one learning before introducing the next all interfere with transfer. The teacher will vary the procedure according to whether she is willing to lose the specifics for the sake of the generalization.

. . . IN THE CLASSROOM

The teacher, then, has to decide whether the transfer in combining two learnings will be positive or negative. Can the learning be merged with others for the sake of a broader concept? If so, the learnings may well be taught together for the sake of reinforcement. Or must the learning be kept intact just as it is taught? If so, any similar learning should be kept away from it in context, time, and teaching procedure.

When a child is working on "there" on a reading chart, the teacher will exert every effort to keep "where" off the charts immediately following. She will repeat the "there" until the child is sure of it. When he is trying to spell "friend" she will avoid saying anything about the rule and exceptions to it, but teach it with such independent cues as she can give.

If a student already writes cursive script well when he comes to a teacher, she will not ask him to change to manuscript or to different slant. If he does subtraction by the additive method she will not insist he learn the take-away procedure. He needs one correct method of using skills, and any one well used is satisfactory.

On the other hand, in teaching social studies there is no advantage in keeping geography, history, anthropology, and political science separate. The student needs to know how people live and adapt to a given environment, and all these subjects are simply different approaches to that broad understanding. He will study a life unit, such as pioneer life, and through it learn why the western routes were placed as they were, how people managed to live on the frontier, why people especially wanted to migrate at a particular period in history, what kind of government they formed as the result of their needs, and how their actions are reflected in our current life. The interweaving of the various social studies strengthens the understanding of each one since the relationships are more important than independent memory for any one.

IMPLICATIONS

These principles mean that the teacher will:

1. Emphasize generalization where the relationship between two learnings is more important than either learning independently. Bring the two learnings together in time, place, mode of presentation, context, meaning and set. Make the classroom as much like the transfer situation as possible. Emphasize similarities, relationships, and comparisons. Stress generalizations and broad concepts. Introduce both learnings together, interweave them in teaching, and constantly vary the structure of each. Teach for conscious transfer through analysis of methods, principles and applications.

2. Isolate each learning that must remain independent and distinct. Separate the learnings that may be confused, in time, place, mode of presentation, context, set, and meaning. Teach one learning completely before introducing the second. Plan a time lapse between the two learnings. Stress the independent meaning of each learning, and avoid varying the structure of either. Avoid comparisons, pointing out relationships, and generalization.

EXERCISES IN APPLICATION

1. Judy found she remembered more when studying for finals if she went to bed immediately after studying. Why was this superior to reviewing for another final? To preparing the next day's work in a related field? Going to a movie?

2. What is occurring when a child substitutes "right" for "write" and "might" for "mite"? What is the best way to help him straighten out his spelling?

3. A study in the field of positive transfer used two groups of children to compare the effect of a "generalization" method of teaching and a "drill" method. In each situation, testing included both a measure of recall of facts and one of ability to use facts in new contexts. How would you expect the methods of teaching to compare on recall of facts? On ability to use facts in new contexts? Which method would you expect to be superior on delayed recall?

4. Mrs. Simpson, a third-grade teacher, is teaching for transfer in her social-studies unit on Indian life. What should she emphasize? How to study a particular people? Generalization? A critical attitude? Particular customs? Why?

5. The most common transfer agents are modes of attack, sets to perform, and general principles. Which agent is acting primarily in transferring high-school physics to repairing a lamp cord at home? In transferring learning of French to learning of Spanish? In transferring arithmetic problem solving to planning a sail for a boat? In transferring a liking for music to a decision to attend a concert?

6. Suppose you were trying to teach the concept of "the greatest good for the greatest number" to a twelfth-grade civics class. How would you approach the concept for the maximum retention? Through slogans? Historical incidents and current events? Other methods? Why? What is the key learning concept?

7. Karen, Laura, and Mary are learning to bowl. Karen has read a book on bowling; Laura has watched the game many times; Mary played dodge ball and similar games when she was younger. Assuming roughly equal mental and physical ability, which will make a more rapid start in bowling? Why?

8. English statesmen in the nineteenth century often came from a background of education in the classics, with the inference that study of the classics trains statesmen better than study of other fields. Analyze the argument, and identify the learning principle to which it is related. Can you think of any possible evidence of the same type of thinking in the modern elementary school?

9. How do research findings on the relation of transfer to the teaching of languages and spelling differ from those concerning other fields? What is the effect of transfer in these subjects? Are there other comparable subject fields?

10. Are positive and negative transfer two different mental processes? In what respects are they the same and in what ways do they differ?

SUGGESTIONS FOR FURTHER READING

Coladarci, A. P. "Educational Psychology." *Ann. Rev. Psych., 9,* 189–212, 1955. A somewhat technical presentation of the field of educational psychology, including motivation, learner characteristics, problem solving, and transfer.

Craig, R. C. "Learning: I. Understanding, Transfer and Retention." *Rev. Educ. Res., 28,* 445–458, 1958. A three-year review of studies of learning, including level of aspiration, praise and reproof, learner activity, knowledge of results, distribution of practice, retention, and transfer.

Ellis, H. *The Transfer of Learning.* New York: Macmillan, 1965. An overview of studies of transfer, including an extensive bibliography.

Gagné, R. M. "The Acquisition of Knowledge." *Psych. Rev., 69,* 355–365, 1962. An analysis of productive learning as transfer from component learning sets to a new activity incorporating those capabilities.

Johnson, D. M., and R. P. Shatton. "Evaluation of Five Methods of Teaching Concepts." *J. Educ. Psych., 57,* 48–53, 1965. A study of the effectiveness of five learning methods in achieving transfer.

Kendler, H. H. "Learning." *Ann. Rev. Psych., 10,* 43–88, 1959. A somewhat technical review of learning research, 1957–1958, including drive, reinforcement, retention, and transfer.

Osgood, C. E. "The Similarity Paradox in Human Learning: a Resolution." *Psych. Rev., 56,* 132–143, 1949. A classic presentation of several generalizations based on research on transfer and retroaction, with a rationalization.

Slawecke, N. J., and J. Ceraso. "Retroactive and Proactive Inhibition of Verbal Learning." *Psych. Bull., 57,* 449–475, 1960. A review of studies of retroactive and proactive inhibition from 1941 to 1959, with an enumeration of pressing issues for research.

Underwood, B. J. "The Effect of Successive Interpolations on Retroactive and Proactive Inhibition." *Psych. Monog., 58,* #3, 1945. A classic study of retroactive and proactive inhibition, with an interpretation in terms of a two-factor theory including overlearning and certain intervening variables.

Van de Geer, J. P., and J. F. M. Jaspars. "Cognitive Functions." *Ann. Rev. Psych., 17,* 145–176, 1966. A somewhat technical review of research on concept formation, problem solving, transfer, and related variables.

Appendix

Implications of Psychology of Learning for Teaching[1]

1. *Establish some kind of common purpose at the beginning of each activity.*

1.1. Recognize spontaneous interests; where possible build group interests around them.
1.2. Relate each learning to previous interests.
1.3. Make the purpose clear at the *beginning* of the activity.

2. *Vary the distraction level in the classroom according to the needs of the group and the nature of the activity.*

2.1. Keep the distraction level lifelike.
2.2. Relieve students of unnecessary distractions.

3. *Use forms of motivation that are integral parts of the life situation in which the learning will function.*

4. *Develop long-term interests.*

4.1. Know and use the individual's existing interests.
4.2. Develop new interests by introducing new experiences and making them satisfying.

1 This summary of chapter conclusions may be used as a method for identifying principles in the study questions at the end of each chapter, or for identifying those observed operating in classrooms during observation assignments.

4.3. Build interests through using physical activity, appeals to the desire for investigation and adventure, social situations, and realism.

5. *Avoid over-motivation through too great intensity or too frequent repetition of a given form.*

5.1. Increase motivation gradually.

5.2. Turn to other motivations before there are signs of disturbance such as turning away from the activity, freezing, excitement, or aggression.

5.3. Discontinue motivation if there is any sign that learning is disrupted.

6. *Help students set their own standards for accomplishment.*

6.1. Avoid imposing goals that are foreign to them.

6.2. Avoid adding to a strong self-imposed motivation.

7. *Help students set realistic goals for themselves.*

7.1. Help the child to know his abilities so that he may choose goals wisely.

7.2. Individualize goals wherever possible.

7.3. Dignify all goals so that each can retain self-respect.

8. *Help students meet the goals they have set.*

8.1. Prevent failure by helping in the selection of suitable goals.

8.2. Build self-respect whatever the achievement may be.

9. *Adapt to the learner's natural tempo of work wherever possible.*

9.1. Do not urge students to hurry or slow down.

9.2. Interrupt the individual's rhythm of work for emphasis only.

10. *Make time scheduling a part of the planning of each activity.*

10.1. Stress quality of work as well as speed.

10.2. Stress work units rather than time units.

11. *Evaluate each learning experience in a suitable way.*

11.1. Make sure the information given is specific.

11.2. Emphasize correct ways of doing things rather than mistakes.

11.3. Give information on accomplishment immediately after learning.

11.4. Use evaluation particularly often with bright students.

12. *Introduce feeling tone only into activities you wish the learner to remember.*

12.1. Ignore behavior you wish him to forget.

12.2. Delay handling strongly emotional problems until the child involved has recovered his poise.

13. *Use negative reinforcement only in activities you want the child to remember, dislike, and avoid.*

13.1. Keep negative feeling tone moderate at all times.

13.2. Follow negative reinforcement by positive suggestion.

14. *Use positive reinforcement in activities you wish the child to remember and repeat.*

14.1. Keep the balance of feeling positive for each individual.

14.2. Arrange situations in which the student can succeed in preference to depending on praise.

14.3. Vary the feeling tone from time to time.

15. *Select the form of motivation that is best for the particular individual.*

15.1. Use positive forms more often with young children, girls, the slow-learning, the maladjusted, and the introverted.

15.2. Use negative forms somewhat more freely with older children, boys, the rapid-learning, the well-adjusted, and the extroverted.

16. *Use the classroom audience to increase the strength of motivation.*

16.1. Avoid over-motivation through use of the audience.

16.2. Avoid using negative forms of motivation before an audience.

16.3. Make sure the learner understands and prepares for his audience.

16.4. Use the audience in lifelike ways.

16.5. Use the audience chiefly when speed is desired.

17. *Use competition chiefly as self-competition against the student's own record.*

17.1. Avoid competition between individuals.

17.2. Avoid over-motivation through competition.

17.3. Make the competition easy enough that the learner can succeed.

17.4. Use competition chiefly where speed or overlearning is important.

18. *Use cooperative group work often.*

18.1. Use group work chiefly with older students.
18.2. Use cooperation for problem solving and where quality of work is important.
18.3. Form groups that are small and homogeneous, follow social attractions, and give students some chance to choose.

19. *Plan carefully for the more capable learner in group situations.*

19.1. Use audience and competitive situations very little.
19.2. Let him work with students of similar ability often.
19.3. Respect his desire for more individual work and self-direction.

20. *Vary the order and context in which material is presented.*

20.1. Ask for recall in a different order or context.
20.2. Use many different sources presenting the same facts.
20.3. Use intensive study only for memorization or exact reproduction.

21. *Use first and last positions in a lesson for overview and emphasis.*

21.1. Use middle positions for elaboration.
21.2. Vary activities so that there are few "middle" positions.

22. *Use material at the learner's normal learning level.*

22.1. Determine each individual's learning potential.
22.2. Avoid giving him tasks that are too long or too complex *for him.*

23. *Choose material that is meaningful for the learner.*

23.1. Present new learnings in a familiar context.
23.2. Build meanings through experience and discussion.
23.3. Encourage the student to look for logical relationships and principles in all types of material.
23.4. Spend relatively large amounts of time developing concepts, relatively little on drill.

24. *Choose learning units that are simply and clearly structured, and follow that structure in presentation.*

24.1. Start by presenting the whole outline.
24.2. Isolate any segments that must be mastered.
24.3. Teach separately units that do not "belong" together.

25. *Try to make each impression vivid.*

25.1. Use contrast in relative size.
25.2. Use color contrast.
25.3. Use movement and development.
25.4. Vary the procedure to retain novelty.

26. *Present material through as many sensory modalities as you can.*

26.1. Encourage the learner to speak as he learns whenever it is appropriate.
26.2. Encourage manipulation of materials for kinesthetic and motor impression.
26.3. Encourage the student to move about as he learns.
26.4. Use pictures, graphs, and maps to help him visualize what he is learning.

27. *Help the learner maintain an active attitude at all times.*

27.1. Define the purposes before the learning starts.
27.2. Stress learning for permanent retention and for use.
27.3. Isolate for attention any specific learning.

28. *Provide for reaction on the part of the learner in every learning situation.*

28.1. Stress discussion, attempted recall, note taking, and questioning.
28.2. Avoid lecturing, passive reading, and too much demonstration.
28.3. Avoid situations that lead to guessing.

29. *Provide just enough help to keep the learner moving ahead.*

29.1. Give help as soon as it is needed.
29.2. Give most of the help early in the learning.
29.3. Give help in a form that requires action on the part of the learner.

29.4. Avoid helping too much, too late, or when the student is busy with his own attempts.

29.5. Give help in positive rather than negative form.

30. *Encourage the learner to solve problems for himself.*

30.1. Encourage him to explore the problem freely at first.

30.2. Give him cues for solution through questions or experience, not through statements or demonstrations.

30.3. Stress skills, attitudes, and processes that will transfer to other problem-solving situations.

31. *Expect some forgetting after every learning.*

31.1. Expect rapid forgetting immediately after learning.

31.2. Expect rapid forgetting of new or formal learnings.

32. *Adapt procedures for preventing forgetting to the kind of use you expect the learner to have for the material.*

32.1. Teach skills to the level of permanent recall.

32.2. Teach most content to the level of recognition.

32.3. Do not bring attitudes and appreciations to the level of recognition.

33. *Provide overlearning to get permanent retention at the level of recall.*

33.1. Limit overlearning to 50 percent of the time needed for mastery.

33.2. Check the accuracy of practice to prevent modification.

33.3. Stop overlearning at any sign of satiation or negativism.

33.4. Use negative practice to block persistent faulty habits.

34. *Stop a learning activity near the point of mastery.*

34.1. Break it as near that point as possible.

34.2. Avoid any implication of failure in the interruption.

35. *Distribute the learning periods to get permanent retention at the level of recall.*

35.1. Make the initial period long enough to review the whole process or material.

35.2. Decrease the length of practice period systematically.

35.3. Adapt the length of rest period to the length of work period.

35.4. Use different and easy activities during the rest period.

36. *Plan to counteract loss in formal skills during the summer vacation.*

36.1. Give special attention to skills that are new and formal.

36.2. Review for a few weeks in the spring.

36.3. Help plan summer activities which use skills and supplement content.

36.4. Review in the fall as a basis for the next year's work.

37. *Emphasize generalization where the relationship between two learnings is more important than either learning independently.*

37.1. Bring the learnings together in time, place, mode of presentation, context, meaning, and set.

37.2. Make the classroom as much like the transfer situation as possible.

37.3. Emphasize similarities, relationships, and comparisons.

37.4. Stress generalizations and broad concepts.

37.5. Introduce both learnings together, interweave them in teaching, and constantly vary the structure of each.

37.6. Teach for conscious transfer through analysis of methods, principles, and applications.

38. *Isolate each learning that must remain independent and distinct.*

38.1. Separate the learnings that may be confused, in time, place, mode of presentation, context, set, and meaning.

38.2. Teach one learning completely before introducing the second.

38.3. Plan a time lapse between the two learnings.

38.4. Stress the independent meaning of each learning and avoid varying the structure of either.

38.5. Avoid comparisons, pointing out relationships, and generalization.

Index